D0114302

COMING OUT RIGHT

COMING OUT RIGHT

The Story of Jacqueline Cochran, the First Woman Aviator to Break the Sound Barrier

Elizabeth Simpson Smith

Walker and Company
New York

First published in the United States of America in 1991 by Walker Publishing Company, Inc.

Published simultaneously in Canada by Thomas Allen & Son Canada, Limited, Markham, Ontario

Library of Congress Cataloging-in-Publication Data

Smith, Elizabeth Simpson.
    Coming out right : the story of Jacqueline Cochran, the first woman aviator to break the sound barrier / by Elizabeth Simpson Smith.
        p.   cm.
    Includes bibliographical references and index.
    Contents: Describes the life of Jacqueline Cochran, who overcame poverty and lack of education to become a world-famous pilot and head of the Woman's Airforce Service Pilots during World War II.
        ISBN 0-8027-6988-8
        ISBN 0-8027-6989-6 (lib. bdg.)
        1. Cochran, Jacqueline—Juvenile literature. 2. Air pilots—United States—Biography—Juvenile literature. 3. Women air pilots—United States—Biography—Juvenile literature.
    [1. Cochran, Jacqueline. 2. Air pilots. 3. Women air pilots.]
    I. Title.
    TL540.C63S55   1990
    629.13'092—dc20
    [B]   90-39649
    [92]   CIP
                                                                         AC

Book Design by Irwin Wolf & Shelli Rosen

Printed in the United States of America

10 9 8 7 6 5 4 3 2 1

For reasons they will understand, this book is lovingly dedicated to members of the Wednesday Writers Workshop (which actually meets on Thursdays).

"Given time enough, everything seems to come out right."
Jacqueline Cochran in her autobiography
The Stars at Noon

CONTENTS

Acknowledgments   xi

One   1

Two   7

Three   13

Four   21

Five   26

Six   31

Seven   37

Eight   42

Nine   50

Ten   57

Eleven   61

Twelve   70

Thirteen   75

Fourteen   83

Fifteen   87

Sixteen   94

Seventeen   100

Appendix   105

    Important Events in Jacqueline Cochran's Career   105

    Other Sources of Information on Jacqueline Cochran   107

    Jacqueline Cochran Exhibits   108

Index   109

Acknowledgments

After Hazel Stroda of the Dwight D. Eisenhower Library became involved in research for this book, she commented that she was "so captivated by Jacqueline Cochran" that she was grateful to be involved in the project. The same spirit of cooperation and excitement surfaced among the many other people who contributed to this book: Kathleen A. Struss of the Dwight D. Eisenhower Library, Claudia M. Oakes and Melissa A. N. Keiser of the National Air and Space Museum of the Smithsonian Institution, Karen Bates of the Clemson University Libraries, Joan Morris of the Florida Department of State, the Women's Army Corps Museum, Miriam Herin, Jean and Claude Harrison, Shirlee Tathwell, Richard Carlson, Ginnie and Mel Bayer, my husband Ed, and my editor Jeanne Gardner. To each I say a big and heartfelt "Thank you."

Photo Credits

Photos of sawmill village courtesy of the Florida Department of State; all other photographs are through the courtesy of the Dwight D. Eisenhower Library.

COMING OUT RIGHT

ONE

When Jacqueline Cochran was six years old she learned a secret so dreadful it filled her heart with fear.

It was a very ordinary day in 1916. Jackie's mother, out of sight, was talking to a visiting friend. Suddenly her voice dropped to a whisper as she told her friend the secret: Jackie was not her "real" daughter, not "one of the family," as she put it. She was raising Jackie for an unknown woman in exchange for a small tract of land some distance away. She was speaking low, not in her usual strident tone, because she had promised that Jackie never would be told.

The words set Jackie's mind whirling. Who were her "real" parents, and why had they abandoned her? Where were they now? Did she have "real" brothers and sisters? And where would she live if her foster parents decided to rid themselves of a daughter that was not "one of the family."

Then a strange feeling of relief washed over Jackie. To learn that she was not "one of the family" gave her a sense of freedom. Although she had never gone to school and her foster parents had spent no time teaching her even the simplest facts, Jackie felt she "knew" certain things. The "knowing," which she later called a sixth sense, came during periods when she felt alone and in need of help. And one of the first things she "knew" was that she didn't want to continue living the way her foster family lived for the rest of her life. Now, with this discovery, she would be free to escape someday.

The secret changed Jackie's life. Everything she did from that day forward was part of a plan to gain independence and improve her life. It was probably at that moment when Jackie's great determination first came into being—the determination to get whatever she set her heart on.

Jackie has been described as "tough as nails." People who knew her as an adult said she behaved outlandishly and created scenes wherever she went. Her emotions climbed and dipped like an airplane and people never knew what to expect. She was comfortable with men who were accomplishing things, and short-tempered with women who did not assume control of their lives.

ABANDONED SAWMILL VILLAGE IN NORTHERN FLORIDA, TYPICAL OF WHERE JACKIE GREW UP.

Yet these same people found her warm, generous, and exciting. Most of the people she met grew to love her. Some merely tolerated her. But all of them admired her for her remarkable accomplishments.

And one thing was sure: anyone who met Jacqueline Cochran certainly would remember her.

Whenever Jackie was asked where she grew up she quickly replied, "Sawdust Road." Her "father" and "brothers" were migrants who traveled from town to town in search of work. At the time that Jackie learned the secret, they were living in a sawmill town in northern Florida. A sawmill town was more like a camp set up around a sawmill on the edge of woods. While trees were being leveled and their logs transported to the mill, laborers migrated to the town. After the woods were depleted and the logs sawed into planks, which sometimes took years, the workers moved on to another sawmill. Jackie's father and brothers were sawmill workers.

There were no paved streets or sidewalks in a sawmill town, only narrow roads and walkways tightly packed with sand. Dogs and cats and chickens and pigs roamed at will. Workers and their families lived in small shacks or shanties with neither running water nor electricity. For light they used a mojo lamp, a hollow stalk of corn stuck into a bottle, with oil as fuel and a scrap of wool for a wick. There weren't even windowpanes in Jackie's home. During winter the windows were stuffed with paper or oilcloth to keep out the cold.

A stove stood in one corner and served for both cooking and heating. There was no table for eating and no set time for meals. The family consisted of two brothers, Joe and Henry, and two sisters, Mamie and Myrtle, all older than Jackie. They all believed in fending for themselves. If there was a pot of beans on the stove, Jackie could walk right in and help herself. If not, she

JACKIE AS A CHILD (RIGHT) WITH SISTERS MAMIE AND MYRTLE, ALL WEARING DRESSES AND SHOES BORROWED FOR THE PHOTO-GRAPH.

had to wander through the pine woods to the scrub brush along the edge of the swamp, on through the marshes and down to the bayou. There she could catch her own mullet, or beg from other fishermen who had already made a catch.

Sometimes Jackie was lucky enough to stalk a stray chicken, bait it with a kernel of corn tied to a string, and leave the bait lying invitingly in a path where the chicken would scratch for food. Jackie would hide behind a bush until the chicken swallowed the kernel, then she'd reel in her catch like a fish. On such days the rare smell of chicken in the pot assured Jackie she would sleep with a full belly that night, an infrequent occasion for the thin, curly-haired blonde who seldom knew a night without hunger. If she felt guilty about stealing a chicken, she comforted herself by saying that the chicken was a thief, too. It stole the kernel of corn.

Jackie described herself as a ragamuffin who was allowed to do exactly what she pleased most of the time. If she didn't show up at dark, no one came looking, not even the time she and two young friends got lost and slept in the woods all night.

Sometimes these things bothered Jackie, especially at night when she lay on her thin pallet on the floor and did some thinking before dropping off to sleep. It didn't seem quite right, all this freedom for a six-year-old, even though she took complete care of herself, seldom asked for anything, and received precious little. In all her life she had never owned a toy or even a pair of shoes. In her mind it seemed that mama was at fault, always fussing and shouting and swatting Jackie and her sisters with a stick of kindling. Maybe hunger pains bothered mama more than they did some people, but Jackie noticed that things were different at other houses. The floors in nearby shacks were swept and there were dishes in the cupboards. Clean sheets and freshly washed clothes appeared on clotheslines with regularity. But every day Jackie wore the same soiled dress, a flour sack with a hole snipped out so it would slip over her head. There was no bathroom for bathing, and Jackie had never even washed her hair.

Now, with her new knowledge, Jackie realized she didn't have to be like mama and the others. She could break away from their mold and someday live in a better world. But even with all her special "knowing," Jackie did not foresee the remarkable experiences that lay ahead.

TWO

During the next few days Jackie began to understand certain mysteries that had puzzled her in the past. For instance, her "mama" had never been able to tell Jackie when her birthday was, nor did she seem to know Jackie's true age. And Jackie even wondered if she would ever learn her own last name. Many years later she found reason to believe that her true name may have been Bessie Lee Pittman and that she probably was born near Muscogee, Florida, between 1908 and 1912, but the information was never confirmed.

She learned that both of her parents died and that she was turned over to foster parents at about age four. Jackie never divulged her foster family's name nor how she came to be called Jacqueline. But many years later, after she left home, she decided suddenly to select another family name. Running her finger down a telephone book, she chose the name Cochran.

Jackie felt less and less like a member of her foster family, and her first thought was to run away. One day a circus came to town, a ragtag carnival with one elephant and a bearded lady. Jackie made friends with the bearded lady, ran errands, and carried buckets of water for the elephant. On the last day she announced to her friend that she was joining the circus and would work for her forever. That night Jackie bedded down on a pile

of straw at the edge of the clearing, away from the tents and
elephant, waiting for the scheduled departure at dawn. But
when she awoke the next morning the circus was gone. All that
was left was her pile of straw and a sack someone had thrown
over her for warmth.

Jackie carried a longing for the circus in her heart the rest of
her life. Once, after she was grown and married, she satisfied
that longing by riding the lead elephant at the opening of the
Ringling Brothers Circus in New York's Madison Square Garden. Her husband had arranged the treat to celebrate Jackie's
recovery from a serious illness.

After the circus left, Jackie pinned her hopes on some gypsies
who camped down the road. Someone had warned her that
gypsies steal children, and Jackie decided to give them the

JACKIE ATOP AN ELEPHANT AT MADISON SQUARE GARDEN,
1938.

chance. She wandered into camp, making herself as visible and as useful as possible. But in time she became a nuisance and the gypsies eventually ran her off.

The only structure to Jackie's life took place once a month when a Catholic priest appeared on Sawdust Road to hold mass. Jackie's foster parents surprised her by instructing her to go—alone. Later she supposed that they were fulfilling a promise made to her biological parents to raise her in the Catholic faith. Jackie found the priest full of goodness, and she went eagerly every month. She remained devoted to the Catholic church the rest of her life.

When school started, Jackie decided to enroll, although no one at home had mentioned it or seemed to care one way or another. On the third day the teacher whipped her with a ruler, and Jackie bolted from the schoolhouse without a backward glance. She felt the teacher was unfair, that she had picked on Jackie because she was a dirty ragamuffin, and she never returned to her classroom.

Every day she watched a slow freight train rattle by her door. In tow was a string of boxcars with words in large letters printed on their sides. Jackie watched the words drift by, wrote them in the sand, and eventually learned the alphabet, gloating that she had learned more from a freight train than from a teacher with a snapping ruler.

The next year a new teacher arrived in the Florida sawmill town, and Jackie decided to slip into the schoolhouse to look her over. Miss Bostwick was the most beautiful woman she had ever seen. Her dress was clean and pretty, and she spoke with the most elegant accent Jackie had ever heard. Miss Bostwick was from Cincinnati, Ohio, a city so far away that it sounded mystical and magic. She decided to stay.

Like the previous teacher, Miss Bostwick was strict and quick to swat any mischief-maker with a ruler. But Miss Bostwick was fair, and that was good enough for Jackie.

After school Jackie lingered, asking questions and drinking in the crisp words that fell from Miss Bostwick's lips. On the second day the teacher offered Jackie a job. She would pay her ten cents a week to bring firewood every day to her boarding-house room. With her heart thumping wildly, Jackie raced to the woodpile, chopped the wood into tiny slivers and carried it gingerly up the steps to the room Miss Bostwick indicated. What she saw was fine enough for a palace. There were curtains at the windows, a coverlet on the bed, and even a screen for Miss Bostwick to dress behind. A pot was simmering on the small cookstove, giving off a mouth-watering fragrance Jackie had never before smelled. At Miss Bostwick's invitation, Jackie tasted her first stewed prunes from that simmering pot. She rolled the plump, sweet fruit from one side of her mouth to the other, savoring its rich taste before allowing it to slide down her throat.

Every day Jackie carried more wood to Miss Bostwick's quarters, and the pile grew so fat that Miss Bostwick cried "enough." But Jackie kept on. She wanted excuses to visit the beautiful room and feast on Miss Bostwick's lovely words.

One day Miss Bostwick surprised Jackie with a dress she had ordered from a catalog, Jackie's first store-bought dress. She produced a matching hair ribbon and a comb, and taught Jackie how to wash her hair and bathe. In Miss Bostwick's orderly sanctuary, removed from the squalor and disharmony of her foster family, Jackie felt herself unfolding like a spring daffodil, spreading her petals and opening her inner self to life. She dreaded the arrival of summer and Miss Bostwick's departure for Cincinnati. She feared she would wither and waste away during those long hot months. Even worse, she feared Miss

Bostwick would not return to the sawmill town to teach another year or that her family would move away.

But Miss Bostwick did return and Jackie again became her shadow. Every morning before school she darted to her teacher's house to button her dress. After school she followed her home and, her heart racing, climbed the now-familiar steps to the

EXAMPLE OF JACKIE'S HANDWRITING AS AN ADULT. (GRAPHIC ENHANCEMENT BY KAREN HAYNES)

room that held such magic. Miss Bostwick read aloud to Jackie, teaching her new words. One day she produced a copy of *David Copperfield* and made Jackie sit quietly and read it. During the days that followed, Jackie wrote down the words she didn't understand. At the end of each day Miss Bostwick taught Jackie their meaning and pronunciation and helped her use them in a sentence. Under such privileged tutelage, Jackie felt her mind expand. Her heart swelled with hope for the future.

But the third year Jackie's great fear materialized. Miss Bostwick did not return and Jackie never again went to school. Although she continued reading, she struggled with spelling for the rest of her life, and her scrawling second-grade writing forever filled her with embarrassment. But from Miss Bostwick she gained a larger vision of the world and a hunger for life experiences that never left her. And for the first time she learned to care for someone who truly cared for her. As Jackie said later, Miss Bostwick lifted her horizons and gave her ambition.

Many years later Jackie traveled to Cincinnati in search of Miss Bostwick, but every trail led to a dead end.

THREE

The lifestyle of Jackie's foster family, dreary as it was, had a rhythm of its own, a flow of ups and downs as predictable as ocean waves. A time or two, when business was greatly improved, they moved from their shack to company-owned houses in larger towns. One time Jackie's pallet on the floor was replaced with a St. George bed. Although a St. George bed was only a shelf of rough boards built out from the wall and supported by two legs under the outer edges, it was a luxury and provided safety from rats that scurried across the floor at night. Sometimes Jackie had a thin mattress or blanket to cover the boards. In one town there were even electric lights strung along two or three blocks of the main street, although inside the houses the only light trickled dimly from kerosene lanterns. Compared to mojo lamps, these lanterns represented great wealth to Jackie.

With time on her hands, Jackie roamed the streets and discovered something very pleasing about herself. In her words, people "took to her like an unusual or striking-looking wild animal that wanders into camp to be fed and cared for." They paused whatever they were doing and talked with her, looking her squarely in the face. Was it her honesty, her openness? Her curiosity and eagerness to learn? Her boundless energy and the way she jumped right in and helped, whatever the task at hand?

Or did they feel sorry for her, a barefoot ragamuffin in tattered clothes? Perhaps she'd never know, but Jackie vowed she would change her image. When anyone asked what she wanted to be when she grew up, Jackie replied almost breathlessly, "I'm going to have fine clothes and an automobile and be rich and see the world."

Although she had no specific plan, Jackie's goal was independence. Whenever a door opened, she would march right through it with the same enthusiasm as when she had climbed the stairs to Miss Bostwick's quarters. And she planned one day to open a few doors herself. But first she had to grow up.

Jackie, although scarcely more than eight years old, soon found a way to grow up even more quickly than she had imagined. The women in Sawdust Road who were expecting babies had no choice but to give birth at home. Hospitals were expensive and located some distance away, and sawmill workers had no cars or other means of transportation. Most of the women had other small children to care for alone, for their husbands were required to work fourteen or more hours a day. Since Jackie didn't go to school, they hired her to live with them and help out several days before and after giving birth.

Jackie took the jobs with enthusiasm for they provided a few days away from home and her second chance to earn money. She rose at dawn. Standing on a box so she could reach the stove, she prepared breakfast and got the men off to work. Afterward she swept the house, took care of the other children, and tended the mother. Her pay was ten cents a day.

On one assignment Jackie learned about life very quickly. The woman was only seventeen years old and alone. Her young husband was away on a logging trip deep in the woods. The woman's labor pains started early one evening just as storm clouds, roused to a fury by wind whipping in from the gulf, set rain thundering on the roof and beating against the flimsy walls. At first she told Jackie to fetch a neighbor. Then, fearing that Jackie would get lost in the woods, she changed her mind. "I'll be all right till daybreak," she assured her. But later that night the baby came. Jackie served as midwife, boiling water and following the woman's instructions until the thin cry of a newborn filled the shack with a sound Jackie had never heard before. It was a night she never forgot.

The kitchens in these shacks became a source of pleasure. Unlike her "mama's" kitchen, they were stocked with food and supplies, although simple, and for the first time Jackie had a chance to cook something other than a pot of beans or a stolen chicken. During this period she developed a talent for cooking. Throughout her life she found great pleasure in preparing spur-of-the-moment meals for her friends. But she had no patience for food not prepared correctly and with care. When dining in elegant restaurants later in her life she often embarrassed friends by storming into the kitchen and loudly scolding the chef.

During her time off, Jackie strolled to the mill commissary. With her face pressed against the showcase glass, she eyed a doll she wanted more than anything in the world. The doll was not for sale, but lottery tickets for a drawing just before Christmas were being given away with every twenty-five-cent purchase. The person with the lucky number would win the doll.

By Christmas Jackie had earned four dollars working for the new mothers, enough for sixteen chances on the doll. But times were bad and she hadn't been paid even a penny. She made the rounds of Sawdust Road in search of other jobs. She drew water from the well for women to do their washing, and lugged the buckets to their houses. The ropes on the well rubbed her hands almost raw, but when the day of the drawing arrived Jackie had earned fifty cents, the price of two tickets. On Christmas Eve one of her tickets was drawn. The doll was hers.

But Mama and Papa had other ideas. Jackie's older sister now had a two-year-old baby named Willie Mae, and Jackie's foster parents took the doll from Jackie and gave it to Willie Mae. "You're too old for a doll, anyway," they said. Jackie was heartbroken and vowed some day she would right the wrong. Years later when Willie Mae was grown and had a child of her own, Jackie moved them to New York City to give them a new and better way of life. But she made one stipulation: Willie Mae was to surrender the doll. Jackie kept the lottery-ticket doll the rest of her life as a reminder that wrongs need to be righted and that, given enough time, everything can turn out right.

The "bad times" that prevented Jackie from being paid the four dollars she had earned actually opened new doors for her. Her parents heard that Columbus, Georgia, had become a boomtown where anyone could get a job in a textile mill. The foster family packed up their few belongings and prepared to say goodbye to Sawdust Road forever. They walked three miles to Panama City to catch a train to what promised to be a new tomorrow. But, without the price of tickets, they had to ride in the caboose with the railroad crew. When the steam engine ran out of fuel, Jackie and her family had to alight and help the railroad workers pick up pine knots to fire the engine for another few miles. They arrived in Columbus just before dark and rode an open streetcar through town and out to a dreary mill village. This time their house was bigger, with electricity and running water and even an indoor bathroom, the first Jackie had ever seen. Their furniture consisted of mattresses on the floor and a cookstove bought on credit. But Jackie, still less than ten years old, sensed a great change was taking place, that her life never again would be the same.

Since there were no laws to keep children from working and no labor union at the textile mill to govern the hours, Jackie immediately took a job. She was paid six cents an hour to work from six o'clock in the evening until six o'clock in the morning. Her job was to deliver bobbins by pushcart up and down the long aisles. On each side of the aisles large weaving looms clanged and clattered louder than a freight train. Jackie was not as tall as the cart she pushed, so she burrowed a little pathway down the middle of the bobbins. On tiptoe she then could see through the opening and guide her cart.

Working conditions at the mill were appalling. Lighting inside the large, dark rooms was dim, and ventilation was poor. Cotton lint floated in the air like drifts of dingy snow. Jackie breathed this cotton dust into her lungs and tasted it on her tongue. By the time six o'clock rolled around, her face was gray with it. Spinning frames and looms clanged and rattled all night. There was no rest room and no place to sit even for a moment.

Jackie was permitted thirty minutes off at midnight for supper, but she often crawled into her cart and slept a few minutes. One night she was awakened when a foreman pinched her "in a way no woman should be pinched," she said later. Jackie balled up her fist and hit the foreman squarely in the nose. She wasn't bothered again.

The first week Jackie earned four dollars and fifty cents, which Mama promptly snatched from her. Before the next payday Jackie made a deal with her mother—she gave her three dollars and kept a dollar and a half for herself, an arrangement she felt was fair. Her first purchase was a pair of shoes, the first she had ever owned, which she bought from a street peddler at fifty cents down, fifty cents a week. Eager to grow up, she selected a pair of high heels. But she soon learned she couldn't push a cart all night in heels, so the next week she made a down payment on a pair of sneakers.

Soon she bought a dress-up outfit to wear with high heels—a black woolen skirt with a blouse made of a fabric called *georgette*, a thick crepe with a pebbly surface. Jackie said later she must have looked like a midget clown strolling up and down Broad Street on Sundays, her only day off, gazing at fancy clothes in shop windows and dreaming of a future that seemed more possible every day.

In two months Jackie was given a raise and taught the painstaking task of untangling and refastening loose ends of yarn that caused production to stop. After a while she was promoted to the inspection room, and by the time she was ten years old she was put in charge of fifteen other child workers.

Three years later a labor union was formed at the mill. Jackie paid one dollar for her membership card, although she didn't understand what membership meant. She soon learned. The union called a strike and the mill closed.

Jackie picketed with the rest of the union members. She participated in riots and even threw bricks. "I confess I didn't know what it was about," she said later. "I just wanted my good job back." Every seven days Jackie and her foster family walked to a depot to collect enough beans and fatback to last a week, a gift from the union.

With the mill closed, Jackie again had time to read and think of Miss Bostwick. She chose *Dracula*, Bram Stoker's novel about a blood-sucking vampire. The reason for her choice is not clear, but it was probably one of the few books to which she had access. "It was not a very good book for a ten-year-old to read," she said later, "but I didn't think of myself as a child."

At the end of three months Jackie, always restless, grew disgusted with the strike. She visited her former supervisor and asked what she should do. "Get out of the factory," the woman advised. "You have energy and aims the others don't have. Get a new start."

The supervisor sent her to see a Mrs. Richler, who ran a beauty shop, and told her she would recommend Jackie for a job running errands. Jackie wanted the job so badly that she lied to Mrs. Richler about her talents. She told her she could cook, clean house, and run errands, which indeed she could. Then she bragged about the dexterity of her hands, claiming she could do "anything." Mrs. Richler hired her for a dollar and fifty cents a week, and Jackie moved into the Richlers' nice house. Then Jackie found she had to scramble hard to learn new things in order to live up to her boasts.

The first new thing she learned was to cook kosher food. The Richlers and their six children were orthodox Jews and their food had to be prepared in specific ways. On Sundays the Richlers were not supposed to work, not even to strike a match to light a cookstove, so Jackie had to prepare all meals and do all the work that day. Just as she did when staying with expectant mothers, Jackie learned the cooking procedures quickly and well. Later in life the ability to cook kosher food filled her with pride.

On weekdays Jackie rose at five o'clock, helped with breakfast and the cleaning, then went to the beauty shop to scrub the booths and make up batches of shampoo and hair dye. Mrs. Richler taught her to make wigs, which were called "transformations" and were extremely popular. Soon she was giving shampoos.

As the weeks passed, Jackie thought more and more of her foster home. The rest of the family had returned to Sawdust Road, willingly leaving Jackie behind, and Jackie knew her mother was again struggling through cheerless days without electricity, running water, or regular pay. Jackie's anger gradually dissolved into sympathy, and she began sending half of her pay home every week, a practice she continued until her mother's death many years later.

As Jackie learned more about the beauty business she became increasingly valuable to the shop. The operators worked on commission, so they paid Jackie to help them, thus speeding their work and adding to their income. In time she was earning eight to ten dollars a week.

And eventually, probably without realizing its importance, Jackie learned a procedure that proved to be her long-awaited ticket to independence.

FOUR

Before chemical permanent waves were developed, the only way to curl hair "permanently" was through the use of electricity. The Nestlé electric permanent wave machine was developed in 1904, but it was extremely expensive and few beauticians owned one or knew how to use it. To be permed was a complicated and grueling procedure. The customer sat in a barber-type chair while her hair was being rolled and then wired to an electrical outlet in an overhead dome. Then she had to remain straight and still without tilting her head for hours while the permanent "took." The procedure required nearly all day.

Mrs. Richler owned a permanent wave machine and offered to teach Jackie how to use it. Giving a permanent wave required skill, patience, and an ability to encourage the customer to relax and trust the operator. The fear of overtreated or burned hair hovered in the shop like the fragrance of shampoo. So did the threat of an electrical storm, which would set the entire shop in a frenzy to unplug the machine and "unwrap" the customer. Even though still an adolescent, Jackie was eager to learn, and she tackled the lessons with her customary energy and enthusiasm. Soon she was assisting the other operators, and eventually she was able to give permanents alone.

Now that her work was more profitable, Jackie demanded

that Mrs. Richler not only raise her salary but also relieve her of duties at home. Mrs. Richler reluctantly agreed, and for a year Jackie earned thirty-five dollars a week plus free room and board. Of this she saved every dime she could. Within the year she had saved two hundred dollars, a grand fortune for a young girl at that time.

One day Jackie overheard a beauty equipment salesman tell Mrs. Richler that a department store in Montgomery, Alabama, needed an expert operater for a permanent wave machine. Jackie walked into the room and introduced herself. "I am the expert you're looking for," she said. Jackie got the job.

By now Jackie looked much older than her fourteen years and no longer thought of herself as a child. Moving to another city in another state, a stranger and alone, was more of a challenge than a frightening experience. She walked around a nice part of Montgomery, daydreaming what it would be like to live in such surroundings. Then she saw a house at 12 South Anne Street that she found irresistible. She marched up to the door and knocked. "Will you take me to room and board?" she asked the woman who answered. The woman was horrified and prepared to close the door in Jackie's face. "I've never lived in an elegant home like this," Jackie persisted. "It would be so pleasant to live here with you." The woman sputtered and protested, but her young visitor's pleas won her over. Jackie moved in that day.

Through her landlady, Jackie met young friends, learned to dance, and bought herself a Model T Ford. She was invited to college parties and dances and became quite popular, which Jackie attributed to owning a car. But Jackie never forgot Miss Bostwick's influence. She spent part of every day with books, and by now she was reading the classics. One of her customers, Mrs. Lerton, taught her to sew and crochet so she actually was learning to do "anything" with her hands just as she had boasted to Mrs. Richler.

Because she worked well and fast, Jackie was earning good money. But Mrs. Lerton advised her to enter a nurse's training school at a local Catholic hospital for a career she felt was more promising. Jackie of course could not possibly pass the entrance tests with only a second-grade education, but Mrs. Lerton used her influence to get the young beautician admitted. In order to support herself, Jackie was permitted to work in the hospital while she trained. Her academic grades were poor, but her nursing skills were excellent and she never grew tired of waiting on the sick. On her day off she visited the wards where the poor people were bedded. She cut their hair and shaved the male patients free of charge.

When it came time to take the state board examination in order to become a registered nurse, Jackie's fear about written tests rose to taunt her. Afraid that she wouldn't pass, she left the hospital and took a job for three dollars a day with a country doctor in a sawmill section of Florida. Jackie, forever haunted by the needs of people in sawmill villages, once commented that she felt like Florence Nightingale as she returned to see again the life she had left behind. But her enthusiasm and zeal soon vanished. She found the doctor overworked, his office filthy, and his surgical instruments rusty and dirty. She guessed that he, too, had come to the village with high hopes of helping and improving, but the ever-present squalor dashed his dreams. He simply did what he could.

After only a week the two were called to the woods about fifteen miles from town. They traveled to the site by logging train and found that a man's leg had been crushed beyond repair in an accident. It would have to be removed. There was no way to move the patient to a hospital, so surgery had to take place on the spot. Jackie boiled water in an old tub to sterilize the instruments and helped with the amputation. Afterward she stayed behind four days. Constantly worried that the patient wouldn't survive, she slept in a chair so she could attend him both night and day. Despite the primitive and unsanitary setting, the patient survived and Jackie returned to town.

A short time later Jackie was summoned to a shack to deliver a baby in the doctor's absence. What she saw when she arrived stirred up the bleakness of her own childhood: a St. George bed, pallets on the floor, a mojo lamp, and three small children fending for themselves. Upon delivering the baby she discovered there wasn't even a blanket in which to wrap it. Coming face to face again with people who probably never would improve their lives plunged her into despair. It occurred to her that she was not making them happy but only patching them up so they could continue to live in squalor. That day she resigned her job.

Jackie set out for Pensacola, Florida, the closest city, and got a job at a new beauty shop. As a hairdresser she could at least make women feel good about themselves. To be able to send them away happy made her feel worthwhile.

The shop was shabbily furnished, so Jackie invested part of the money she had saved, became a partner and bought better equipment. But her partner was cheerless and ill-tempered, and Jackie quickly became disenchanted. She answered a newspaper ad and found a job traveling the southeast states selling dress patterns and fabric to dry goods stores.

Again Miss Bostwick's influence touched her life. Driving along in her Model T, Jackie improved her spelling by studying road signs. At night she read books in her hotel room. With a dictionary at her side, she sought new words, which she called "diamonds." The next day her conversation would sparkle with those diamonds, and she used the words over and over until they became a part of her vocabulary. Later she laughingly said that the simplest rules of grammar would escape her and she would revert to the language of Sawdust Road at embarrassing moments, but she always felt comfortable when she spoke "four-bit" words.

Just as her passion for words never ended, neither did her passion for traveling to new cities and meeting new people. Even strangers responded to her friendliness, and from them she learned and stored information, which she called her "formal education." But peddling dress patterns held no future and Jackie soon returned to the beauty business. Eventually she felt the time was right to sell her car and move to the biggest and most challenging city of all—New York. And there a chance meeting opened the door to the career that eventually brought her fame and fortune.

FIVE

In New York Jackie found a cheap room in the back of a kitchen near Broadway and 79th Street. She tacked felt around the door to seal off cooking odors, then set out to find a job. As usual her sights were high. She first applied to a posh beauty salon, Charles of the Ritz, but stormed out the door when the owner demanded that she cut her hair and wear it in the short fashion of the day. Antoine's Salon at Saks Fifth Avenue made no such demands. Antoine was the current rage in New York, and his salon overflowed with customers wanting to be bobbed and permed in the latest styles. He needed someone with Jackie's experience, and she was hired.

Jackie, now about twenty years old, had blossomed into a beautiful young woman. She stood five feet eight inches tall with long blonde curls, chocolate brown eyes, and a trim figure. Her well-to-do customers invited her to parties and she began meeting people. She went dancing several nights a week. Still she found time to read and even do needlework.

In short order Jackie was making good money. She sent a portion to Mama, saved a portion, and invested the rest in cheaper beauty shops in sections of New York less glamorous than Fifth Avenue. During the winter season she was sent to the Antoine salon in Miami Beach to serve her New York customers who wintered there.

JACKIE AT ABOUT AGE TWENTY.

Miami Beach at the time was just coming into its own as a haven where wealthy northerners could bask in its warmer tropical beauty during the cold northern winter months. These part-time inhabitants appeared to thrive on a glittering social season, attending extravagant parties and hosting events of their own. Jackie heard firsthand of these events through her customers, many of whom seemed to talk of nothing else. When an extra woman was needed to round out a party, Jackie was frequently invited. In 1932 one of these invitations, this time to a fancy yacht club for a lavish dinner party, proved to be the most meaningful evening in her life.

Floyd Odlum, son of a Methodist minister from the Midwest, was invited to the same party. Sandy-haired and sedate, he was one of the most sought-after men on the Miami scene. Floyd had earned his first money picking berries, spraying vegetables, and digging ditches. After high school he approached the University of Colorado and promised to repay the money if they would let him attend free. They accepted his offer. Floyd graduated from the University of Colorado Law School in 1915. That same year he passed the state bar examination with the highest grade in the group. Now he was a prominent Wall Street lawyer and a successful investor and industrialist who appeared to have a sixth sense when it came to making money. He was separated from his wife, had two young sons in New York, and frequently had to visit Miami on business.

When inviting Floyd to the party, his host had mentioned the dazzling socialites and actresses who would attend. Floyd declined, saying he was tired and would prefer resting in his hotel room. Then his host mentioned a pretty girl who worked in a shop, and Floyd changed his mind. He would join the party, he said, but only if he could be seated by the shop girl. He wanted to talk with someone down to earth for a change.

Jackie, unaware of the arrangement, spotted Floyd as he entered the clubhouse. "Why can't you invite men like him to your dinner parties?" she chided her host, her gaze following the thin, clean-cut Floyd as he deposited his coat at the checkroom. Moments later Jackie and Floyd were seated side by side as they ate the sumptuous food. Jackie found Floyd, about fourteen years older, to be serious, quiet, and a good listener. She said later she "talked his ears off." She confided to him that she felt trapped working in a salon all day and was bored with the dull conversations of her customers. She was considering looking for a job selling cosmetics across the country. Floyd's reply startled her. With so much competition, he said, she would need wings to cover the territory fast enough.

Later that evening Jackie watched Floyd quietly lose three hundred dollars in the casino and felt sorry for him. He was a bank clerk on holiday, she suspected, and could not afford such a loss.

Two days later Floyd surprised Jackie with an invitation to a party at a swank country club. It was then that she learned her new friend was one of the wealthiest men in the country. After the party Floyd left promptly for New York but told Jackie he would contact her when she returned north.

Employees at Antoine's were not permitted personal telephone calls during business hours. But when Jackie returned to New York two months later she threatened to resign if she were not summoned to the phone if Floyd should call.

He called on May 11. At dinner that night Jackie told him that this was the day she had selected to be her birthday. He honored the occasion by giving her a twenty-dollar gold piece he carried in his pocket. Jackie still had the coin safely tucked in her lockbox at the time of her death.

After that evening Jackie's life was never quite the same.

Floyd's remark about "needing wings" buzzed in her mind like propellers and she turned her thoughts to aviation. At the time, aviation was only a fledgling industry but it already had captured the enthusiasm of the American people. Five years earlier, in 1927, Charles Lindbergh had made his heralded solo flight across the Atlantic Ocean. The U.S. government was now contracting with private companies to carry air mail, and commercial passenger service was just coming into its own. Yet aviation remained a strange combination of part sport, part business. Private citizens who flew were either wealthy enough to own their own planes or were daredevil pilots willing to risk their necks in thrilling air shows. Jackie, always ready to pioneer the new and daring, was intrigued. Floyd's comment may have been made in jest, yet Jackie took it seriously.

That summer she used her accumulated three weeks' vacation and all the money she had saved and signed up for flying lessons at Roosevelt Field on Long Island. At that precise moment in the summer of 1932, Jackie said later, "a beauty operator ceased to exist and an aviator was born."

Jackie's instructor was skeptical that she could learn to fly in only three weeks. But the thought of failing never entered Jackie's mind and she attacked the lessons with determination. On the third day she soloed. Then Jackie grew fearful about passing the written test at the end of her lessons and persuaded her instructor to test her orally. A friend, Micky Rosen, tutored her long hours in the evening from the written material, and in two and a half weeks Jackie had her license.

SIX

With her usual impatience, Jackie, now about twenty-two years old, could hardly wait to try her wings. She resigned her job, borrowed money to rent a Fairchild airplane, and set out for an air meet in Canada. Like a gypsy she planned to follow rivers and lakes to her destination. But navigating was more difficult than she had imagined. When she was forced to stop for a quick course in compass-reading, she realized how inexperienced she was.

But flying was in Jackie's blood. Encouraged by Floyd, she used her savings to drive cross-country to southern California, where she would have a longer flying season than in New York. She bought an aged Travelair plane with a Gypsy engine for $1,200 and took flying instructions from Ted Marshall, a Navy pilot stationed at Long Beach. Ted gave her a stiff course that Jackie suspected was equal to training for the U.S. Navy. She studied Morse code and celestial navigation. And she practiced flying over and over again. Night flying. Day flying. Flying in bad weather. Flying on sunny days. Blind flying. Anything to keep her in the air.

Jackie realized that there were two roadblocks to becoming a topflight pilot, and she was never one to settle for second best. One roadblock was experience. The second was money, for flying was expensive. There was yet a third roadblock she had not anticipated—being a woman.

Jackie soon learned of a way to make money. Air racing! Air racing at the time was equivalent to the Olympics or the Kentucky Derby in popularity and paid handsomely to the winners. Fliers who raced were thought to be glamorous, and the winners became famous overnight. A single win could catapult a pilot to instant financial success through public appearances or endorsements of products.

Air racing held other attractions for Jackie. In fact, it was just her cup of tea—fast, challenging, dangerous, and competitive. And there was another ingredient she always found compelling—a chance to visit new and distant places.

Jackie borrowed money from Floyd and other friends to gain the air experience she needed. First she took four months of intense instruction on instrument flying, and soon she was flying coast to coast entirely on instruments. Then she gained as many hours in the sky as she could. One way was doubling as an airline hostess. At the time there were no hosts or hostesses on commercial airlines. Co-pilots had to serve meals and look after passengers. Most of them hated this part of their job, so Jackie offered to serve as hostess in return for the privilege of piloting the plane a few hours after the passengers fell asleep. The cabins were not pressurized, and passengers often grew nauseated and even blacked out at high altitudes. Jackie had to nurse them and hold bags for their vomit. But she was gaining hours at the controls, and in 1934 she was awarded a commercial pilot's license. It held little value, though, for she quickly learned that only men were allowed to pilot commercial planes.

Jackie, however, was not to be stopped. Her eye was on the 1934 MacRobertson Race from London, England, to Melbourne, Australia, a distance of 12,000 miles. The winner would walk away with $50,000, and Jackie wanted to be that person. Wesley Smith, a commercial pilot and one of the best instrument fliers in the country, consented to be her co-pilot.

Jackie sold her trainer plane for a small profit and borrowed more money to buy a racer. One of her backers during this period was Mabel Willebrandt, a wealthy New York lawyer who was anxious to see women advance.

Jackie learned of a brand new racer—a squat, fast Quod Erat Demonstradum (Q.E.D.) plane called the Gee Bee being prepared by Granville Brothers of Springfield, Massachusetts. "If you can get that plane flown to New York and properly entered in the race, I'll make some sort of arrangements to buy it," Jackie's voice sped through the crackling telephone wires.

The Granville brothers reluctantly agreed. The Gee Bee was far from finished, and they felt the race would be too arduous for a woman. But the male pilot for whom they were preparing the plane had backed out. They were hoping the military would buy it and they needed a pilot to prove its worth. In the end they sold Jackie the Gee Bee and offered her a royalty on all other Gee Bees of the same design sold after the race, precisely the arrangement Jackie needed.

The Gee Bee was rushed to the docks of New York and loaded onto a giant steamship setting sail for England. In tow were two mechanics who were to continue working on the plane for the full two weeks it would take to cross the Atlantic. While the mechanics worked feverishly in the hold of the ship, Jackie stood on deck with her co-pilot, Wesley Smith, and stared hopefully at the sky.

The ship landed in England one week before the scheduled race, but the Gee Bee still was unfinished and untested, and Jackie had yet to fly it for the first time. She rented a hangar, and the mechanics continued preparing the craft.

Finally, thirty-six hours before starting time, Jackie and Wesley climbed into the cockpit and flew to Mildenhall Field near London, where the race would begin. Wesley took the front cockpit and Jackie, because the rear seat had not been installed, sat behind him on a wooden cracker box.

Aloft the plane belched smoke and flames like an old London chimney. The noise was so great that even their shouts could not be heard, so they had to write notes to each other. It was dusk as the fliers nosed down and touched ground. The plane bounced wildly and Jackie feared they had snapped a wing. Newsmen with cameras and note pads waited on the tarmac, eager for an interview with this new female pilot. "We can't let them see the damaged plane," Jackie protested to Wesley. Smiling broadly, she jumped to the ground and merrily led the newsmen away from the plane and into the pilots' quarters as fast as she could.

Later that night Jackie returned to see the Gee Bee to assess the damage. There was none. The Gee Bee was simply a rough-landing plane and she'd have to learn to live with that reality.

At dawn of the second day, Jackie and Wesley zoomed into the sky for the first leg of the race. They flew across the North Sea and soon the countries of Europe lay below them like a map—Belgium, France, Germany, Austria. The first scheduled stop was to gas up at Bucharest, Romania, about 1,400 miles from their starting point. As they approached the Romanian border a thick fog rose to meet them. Beyond the fog lay the treacherous Carpathian Mountains.

Jackie began her climb. The quick ascent almost exhausted the fuel in tank one, and Jackie shifted the fuel flow to the second tank. The engine coughed, sputtered, and died. Jackie now could hear the wind rush past the wings as the plane lost altitude. She switched to tank one again, and the motor started. But for how long? The tank was sure to be almost dry, so Jackie switched again to tank two. The engine stalled. Wesley started to open his canopy, signaling with his hand for Jackie to jump. Jackie tugged at her canopy, but it was stuck fast. Her fingers numb with cold, she worked the switches, clicking them from "Off" to "On" and back to "Off" again. Suddenly the engine wheezed and coughed, then settled into a smooth roar. Jackie pulled back on the stick, and the plane climbed majestically and scaled the mountain. In their haste, the manufacturers had mislabeled the fuel switches. When the valve read "On" it really meant "Off."

Stunned but relieved, Jackie prepared the approach to Bucharest while Wesley worked loose the stubborn canopy over her head. Jackie eased down to the runway and dropped her wing flaps. But one flap was stuck. The plane, now out of balance, wobbled like a drunken turkey. Jackie climbed and circled the field again to give Wesley time to tug at the flap release. Again they came in for a landing, and again the flap held fast. "You can bail out if you want to," she scribbled to Wesley, "but I'm going to take this plane to the ground."

"I won't go if you won't," Wesley wrote back. Finally Wesley wrote, "You're a fool."

"It's my airplane and my life," Jackie zipped back.

On the third sweep both flaps miraculously dropped into position. By then their speed was much too fast for a landing but they were running out of gasoline and would have to take a chance. Jackie nosed the plane down, set the wheels on the edge of the runway and tried to brake. The brakes refused to hold. The plane sped forward and finally rolled to a ragged stop at the far end of the field.

Waiting to greet them was Radu Irimeseu, the Assistant Secretary of State for the Romanian Air Ministry. They had landed on a restricted military airport and the Romanian government wanted to check their credentials!

To Jackie's consternation, the race was over. To repair the

flaps and get the engine back in working order would take hours. Jackie, always a little superstitious, believed in signs. Was this a sign she should give up racing?

As she walked away from the plane, her legs limp from her brush with death and aching from the cramped cockpit, her mind already whirled with plans. Later she learned she was $20,000 in the hole, but Curtiss Wright, manufacturer of the engine, reimbursed her for part of the tab and her friend, Mabel Willebrandt, helped with the rest.

When the results were tallied, Jackie discovered that she had led the entire pack on the first leg of the race.

WESLEY SMITH, RADU IRIMESEU, AND JACKIE IN ROMANIA.

SEVEN

The next scheduled international race was a year off, and Jackie would need every minute of that time. The Bendix, the most prestigious air race of all, would be flown on a cross-country course from Los Angeles, California, to Cleveland, Ohio. This time she would be flying solo.

Jackie now was combining flying with her cosmetic business. In 1935, with Floyd Odlum's help and encouragement, she founded the Jacqueline Cochran Cosmetic Company and set up a laboratory in Roselle, New Jersey, and a rented office in New York. Just as Floyd suggested, she did use an airplane in her business, zipping across the country to call on department stores. With excellent employees and her customary drive to reach the top, she soon was producing quality products and earning a good profit. But she had no intention of giving up racing.

Jackie borrowed money and bought a rebuilt Northrop Gamma equipped with a new air-cooled Pratt and Whitney engine. Arriving in Los Angeles weeks in advance, she spent hours every day testing and growing familiar with her plane. Again, repairs and improvements were being made right up to the moment of departure to make the plane as fast and durable as possible.

Although no woman had ever participated in the Bendix,

both Jackie and Amelia Earhart, whom Jackie had met through mutual friends, turned in applications. Amelia in 1932 had become the first woman to fly solo across the Atlantic and had already made a name for herself. To the women's dismay their applications were declined with the notation, "Men only."

"I can't give up," Jackie argued. "If I concede on this, women will be barred from racing for years, maybe even forever."

She drew up a *Statement of Waiver* and personally visited every pilot who would fly in the Bendix. She argued, coaxed, and pleaded. Finally the men relented and signed an agreement allowing Jackie and Amelia to enter the race.

Drowsiness, hunger, and fatigue would be constant threats in a nonstop air race, so Jackie trained like a prize-fighter. She ate a diet rich in protein to build up stamina, and exercised daily to strengthen her shoulder and arm muscles. Since she would be taking off after midnight, she rearranged her sleep pattern. Every day she went to bed an hour earlier until at last she was retiring at noon. By night she practiced night flying and by day she worked on instrument approaches and landings. On the day of the race, since there would be no bathroom on the plane, Jackie began dehydrating herself by not drinking fluids. Male racers could carry "service tubes" and relieve themselves in flight, but there was no such apparatus for women.

The race was scheduled for August 31, 1935. On August 30 Jackie received a telephone call with an ominous message. The plane had developed a bad vibration. "It's too dangerous to fly," the Northrop engineer warned.

But Jackie refused to cancel. After the furor she had created so she and Amelia could enter, she dared not drop out. She would at least take off, just to prove a point.

That evening a heavy fog rolled over the Los Angeles airport, and the fliers had to wait for intermittent patches of clearing.

Takeoff would have to be made on instrument rather than sight, and instrument takeoffs were particularly hazardous on the short runways used then.

Amelia and most of the other fliers had set out earlier in the evening, and Jackie was there to see them off. Her own flight was postponed to 4:22 A.M. She shouted goodbye to the pilot scheduled to depart just before her and watched him roar down the runway and disappear in the mist. Then a distant explosion jarred her, and a bright, blinding light pierced the fog. Jackie jumped into her car and followed the fire truck down the runway. But by the time the flames were extinguished, the pilot was dead. The twisted wreckage of his plane had to be towed from the runway to make way for the next takeoff—Jackie's.

The sight unnerved her. To appear nonchalant she walked into the airport restaurant and ordered a bowl of chili. An official with the Civil Aeronautics Administration, a government agency, insisted that she abandon her flight. "It's suicidal," he said. "You'll be killed, too."

"Then I'll come back and haunt you," Jackie quipped. This brought laughter from the onlookers and boosted Jackie's spirits. With her head high, she called out a cheery goodbye and left the building. A few moments later she ducked behind the hangar and vomited.

Warming the engine of her plane, Jackie wondered if she was doing the wise thing. She alighted, went inside the airport, and called Floyd in New York. But Floyd, who was now her fiancé, told her there was a fine line between making a choice based on logic and one determined by an emotional drive. In the end, he pointed out, such a decision involves a personal philosophy of life. "No one," he said, "can make that decision for another."

Jackie hung up the phone and rushed back to the plane, her spirits once again soaring. Her decision would stand firm.

Inside the cramped cockpit she barely had space to breathe and no room to change positions. Every inch was filled with essential equipment. Even the masts and wires for the radio had been brought inside the canopy to reduce any outside resistance that would slow her speed. Moving gingerly, Jackie snapped on her helmet and oxygen mask, buckled her seat belts, and checked the wires connecting her to the radio. Her map, carefully marked so she could fly without sight of earth or sound of radio if necessary, was strapped to her knee. Behind her stood the extra tank of gasoline. A box nearby held a soda bottle containing drinking water. The bottle was only half filled to keep it from bubbling over at high altitudes, and was topped with a straw so she could sip without removing her oxygen mask. Small lollipops, her only food, were tucked inside a pocket of her flying suit. But there would be little time or thought for food or drink. Both feet would be busy on the pedals. One hand would control the stick, and the other must remain free to handle the throttle and radio, change gas connections, and even flip the pages of the map.

The ground temperature was stifling, and perspiration trickled down Jackie's neck. She zipped open the special ventilating slits in her suit, but before takeoff she would zip them closed again. Once she gained altitude the outside temperature would plummet below zero and the cockpit would grow frigid.

Shortly after four o'clock Jackie received clearance and roared down the runway, a fire truck and ambulance trailing close behind. In a blind takeoff using only instruments, she barely cleared the outer fence but ripped off the radio antenna trailing below the belly of the plane. She climbed through the fog and gained enough altitude to clear the 7,000-foot mountains that lay inland. And Jacqueline Cochran was on her way.

Around daybreak Jackie encountered a violent electrical storm as she approached the Grand Canyon. The engine was overheating and that, along with a vibrating plane, could mean disaster. This time Jackie made a decision based on logic. The nearest airport was Los Angeles, the one she had just left, so she turned back. When asked what happened, she told the news reporters that she had grown tired and just quit. After all, she reasoned, why place the blame on a faulty plane when she had been told in advance that it needed more work?

More important, her point had been made. Women now were officially eligible for the Bendix. Amelia, Jackie learned later, came in fifth.

EIGHT

Jackie and Floyd, who was now divorced, wanted to set a date for their wedding, but first Jackie decided there was something she must do. She hired a detective and sent him to Florida to search for her roots. She felt this was only fair to the man who would be her husband and the father of the children they wanted. The detective returned with a sealed envelope containing all the information he had been. able to unearth. Jackie presented the envelope unopened to her fiancé, a note written with poor punctuation scrawled across the front:

> *This is For you Floyd   I have never Read the contents.*
> *You can Burn it or Read as you wish   I Love you very much   Jackie.*

Floyd too chose not to read the findings. He placed the envelope, its back sealed with wax in which a twenty-five-cent coin was imbedded, inside a lockbox for safekeeping. The envelope and its secrets, still unopened and unread, were set afire after Jackie's death many years later.

The small, quiet wedding took place while they were on a business trip in Kingman, Arizona, on May 11, 1936, the day Jackie had selected for her birthday. At first they kept it secret because Floyd intensely disliked publicity, but before many weeks the news appeared in newspapers.

Now the new Mrs. Odlum was able to put behind her forever her yearning for a home. Soon they bought an estate in Connecticut, a Manhattan apartment overlooking the East River in New York, and, best of all, a sprawling ranch on the land she loved. Four years earlier while taking flying lessons on the West Coast, Jackie had fallen instantly in love with the then-raw California desert. With glowing eyes she spoke of coyotes and bobcats that roamed its stretches, of its shifting shades of sand, of yucca and mesquite and smoke trees. Before she left California she made arrangements to buy twenty acres. Later she suggested to Floyd that he visit the desert on his next business trip to California so he could experience the same "glories of nature." Floyd, too, fell in love with the desert and purchased one thousand acres. After their marriage the Odlums discovered that their purchases, until then unknown to each other, lay side by side. The land became the Cochran-Odlum Ranch and Jackie's true home.

And soon Jackie quietly established another home, not for herself, but for orphaned children. The orphanage, located close to their New York apartment, became a model institution and an example of how orphanages should be run.

As Mrs. Floyd Odlum, the gutsy Jackie, who never faltered before a closed door, now found more doors opening to her than she could imagine. With Floyd's wealth and influence and Jackie's growing renown, the Odlums lived and traveled in the rarefied air of the elite.

But wealth and influence did not change Jackie's goals. To gain success was still her driving force. She devoted more time and energy to her growing cosmetic business, moving it to the new and impressive Rockefeller Center on Fifth Avenue. While working at Antoine's in Saks Fifth Avenue, Jackie had watched the construction of this new skyscraper and loathed it for cutting off her view of the sky. Now she was a part of the new landscape and the business successes it represented.

Aviation remained Jackie's first love and she became an active member of the Ninety-Niners, a prestigious organization of women fliers. In the past she had always made an effort to help other female fliers. Now, with Floyd's wealth, she could do even more. While she did not continually declare all-out war to advance women's status, she never missed an occasion to make a point.

Jackie and Floyd partially financed Amelia Earhart's attempted around-the-world flight in 1937. Jackie and Amelia had become fast friends since the Bendix race in 1935. The press often tried to pit one against the other and depicted them as arch rivals and jealous competitors. But, as Jackie explained later, their specialities were at opposite ends of the spectrum. Amelia went for long-distance flights that required pampering the engine. Jackie concentrated on speed records that pushed the engine to extreme limits.

Before leaving for her fatal flight, Amelia spent her final weeks at the Cochran-Odlum Ranch, horseback riding, swimming, and resting. The Odlums then flew to Miami to see Amelia and her navigator, Fred Noonan, off on June 1 aboard her plane, the *Friendship*. On departing, Amelia wore a silk scarf that Jackie had given her, and Jackie clutched Amelia's gift, a small American flag, also silk. On July 2 the Odlums, then back in California, were among the first to be notified when the *Friendship* vanished over the South Pacific. George Putnam, Amelia's husband, joined Jackie and Floyd in Los Angeles as the three anxiously awaited further news.

Jackie, who claimed to have extrasensory powers, felt she "knew" certain things about Amelia's plight. She contended that

AMELIA EARHART AND JACKIE RELAX AT THE RANCH.

the aircraft was still floating and that both Amelia and Noonan were alive. Noonan, she perceived, was unconscious from a skull fracture. Although Jackie had never before heard the word, she mentioned the name *Itasco* and said it was a ship near the scene where Amelia's plane could be found. She also mentioned a Japanese fishing vessel in the same waters. Both the report of the *Itasco* and the location of the fishing vessel were later confirmed as true by research teams. The *Itasco* actually had received Amelia's last radio message. But no more messages, either real or extrasensory, were forthcoming. Two days later a despairing Jackie "knew" that Amelia was dead, and she went to a cathedral to burn a candle for her friend. The futile search continued for two weeks but the true details of Amelia's last flight remain unknown. Because they had failed her when she desperately needed them, Jackie never again used her extrasensory powers except for private messages for Floyd.

Five months after Amelia Earhart's disappearance, the Women's National Aeronautical Association gathered at Floyd Bennett Field on Long Island, NY, for a memorial service, with Jackie Cochran as speaker. On that bitter November day Jackie's words resounded like the reality of her own life: "If her last flight was into eternity, one can mourn her loss but not regret her effort."

Jackie's efforts, of course, continued. In 1938 she shattered famous race pilot Howard Hughes's New York to Miami record by flying the course in a then-dizzying 4 hours and 12 minutes in a Seversky plane. The win triggered a fertile idea in the mind of the plane's manufacturer, Russian-born Alexander P. de Seversky. For years he had been trying to prove to the United States Army Air Corps that his P-35 pursuit plane was the finest fighter anywhere, but the Corps was not convinced. The civilian version, the AP-7, was still untested. If he could persuade the

ALEXANDER DE SEVERSKY AND JACKIE.

dazzling speed queen, Jackie Cochran, to fly it in the 1938 Bendix he was sure to gain the military's attention. Jackie jumped at the chance.

The new plane was delivered to Burbank, California, only two days before the race and, in accordance with contest rules, was promptly impounded before Jackie had a chance to test it. When she took off in the early morning of September 3, it was in a plane that she had never flown and one with a new fuel system she had never tried. Seversky had worked out a design that placed extra fuel tanks in the wings for added distance. Jackie discovered soon after takeoff that the right wing was not feeding properly. She had to fly with the defective wing higher than the other to force the fuel into the left wing and then into the engine. Despite this problem she landed in Cleveland to be declared winner 8 hours, 10 minutes and 31 seconds later. She had averaged slightly under 250 miles per hour for the 2,042-mile nonstop course.

When a race official drove out to the end of the runway to pick up Jackie he found he had a wait. Jackie doused her engine, removed her comb and compact and proceeded to repair her makeup and hair. This routine had become a habit. She always stepped from the plane, no matter how hard the trip, looking as if she had emerged from a beauty shop. The official was dismayed, but he waited. After all, Jacqueline Cochran had just won the most prestigious race in air history. Further, she was the only woman in the race against a field of ten men, and the first woman to win a Bendix.

Jackie was escorted to the platform to receive her trophy from Vincent Bendix, sponsor of the race, then promptly took off for New Jersey to capture a new women's west-east transcontinental record to top her Bendix victory like a dollop of whipped cream. Then she caught the next passenger plane back to Cleveland for the evening festivities. She was met at the airport by police escorts on motorcycles, a tribute fitting her new celebrity status, but she asked them to drive slowly into town. She wanted to sit quietly and savor her new victories.

Jackie had said she would quit racing when she won the Bendix. She didn't. Her competitive spirit kept her saddled to the cockpit. In fact, her Bendix win set off a chain reaction of triumphs that crowded the next three years with victories in speed and altitude. In 1939 she set a new international speed record, became the first woman to make a blind landing, and set a new women's altitude record. And in 1938, 1939, and 1940 she received the prestigious Clifford Burke Harmon Trophy as the outstanding woman flier in the world.

Without question, Jackie now occupied a pinnacle in aviation and her reputation was steadily becoming international.

JACKIE RECEIVING THE HARMON TROPHY FROM ELEANOR ROOSEVELT.

NINE

By 1940 air racing was replaced by a race of another kind, a rush to build more durable and innovative airplanes for the military. With Europe at war, it became imperative for the United States to advance its technology. Volunteers were needed to test new oxygen masks, pressure chambers, and high altitude flying, and Jackie usually was first in line.

Although she gave the appearance of robust health, Jackie was plagued with internal problems that began when she had her appendix removed as a teenager. Adhesions resulting from this surgery troubled her through the years, requiring so many operations that her abdomen eventually became as criss-crossed as a road map. High altitude test flights would often trigger bouts of searing pain and even cause bleeding that sent her rushing to the hospital. But Jackie hardly gave these prospects a thought as she eagerly volunteered. One of the test flights caused a blood vessel in her sinus to burst. The experience proved valuable. It led in part to the pressurized cabins and oxygen masks in use today.

Jackie meanwhile kept her attention riveted to the earth-shattering events developing in Europe. Hitler had just invaded Poland. Now England and France had declared war.

In March 1941 the United States made a commitment to

supply Lockheed Hudson bombers to England. But this presented a problem. All of the English pilots were busy at war and could not spare the time to ferry these planes across the ocean. The answer was to employ civilian pilots.

In late March while attending a meeting in Washington, Jackie fell into a discussion with General H. H. "Hap" Arnold, Chief of the U.S. Army Air Force. He mentioned the need for American civilian pilots, male of course, to help transport these bombers for the British Air Transport Auxiliary. Jackie lost no time in suggesting that women, too, could be recruited. "Why don't you do some of that flying yourself?" General Arnold asked.

The general had a twinkle in his eye, and Jackie knew exactly what he had in mind. In both the United States and England women had been trying to gain approval to fly bombers. The prohibiting argument was the same on both sides of the ocean. Women, the officials declared, were not physically strong enough to handle such heavy aircraft. If Jackie could prove them wrong, women may yet have the opportunity to play a role in wartime flying.

General Arnold's comment was all the encouragement Jackie needed. Flying the bomber to England would have a second benefit. England was already using women pilots to ferry lighter planes inside their country, and this would give Jackie an opportunity to look over the operation.

With her ususal zeal she presented her credentials to the Air Transport Auxiliary (ATA) headquarters in Montreal, Canada, where the ferrying decisions were made. The officials examined Jackie's qualifications, just as they did for men, and approved them. They would call her, they said.

Jackie waited, but no call came. Growing impatient, she enlisted the aid of a high-ranking British friend of Floyd's, Lord

Beaverbrook, who had just been named Minister of Procurement for England. Again she waited.

After six months Jackie finally was summoned to Monteal. Her credentials were fine on paper, the officials assured her, but she would have to submit to new tests in the air.

And Jacqueline Cochran, the woman who had been declared the world's best female flier, had to prove her skill.

"You think you're pretty hot, don't you?" the captain in charge of her flight tests asked.

"I'm good," Jackie replied. She enumerated her experience, but the instructor looked bored and disinterested.

"I'm going to have fun checking you out," he interrupted, chuckling.

The tests lasted three days and were grueling. After the final landing Jackie half-jokingly commented that her arm was sore from so many pulls on the heavy emergency brakes and asked the captain if he would taxi the ship to the hangar. The report that zoomed to Washington stated that Jacqueline Cochran indeed had passed all the tests, but probably would not be able to handle brakes in an emergency. Recommendation: Negative.

The authorities in Washington, however, felt the complaint was trivial and issued official orders permitting Jackie to ferry a Lockheed Hudson bomber from Montreal to Prestwick, Scotland. At that moment, she said later, "hell broke loose." Even though she had been recommended by both General Arnold and Lord Beaverbrook and had passed all tests, she had yet to meet the most formidable foe of all—male pilots!

When they heard the news, the male pilots already flying for the ATA threatened to strike. At a mass meeting, to which Jackie was not invited, they argued that missions were supposed to be secret and they questioned if a famous pilot such as Jackie could escape publicity. She was sure to be shot down by the

Germans, they argued, and the ATA then would be blamed. Some even grumbled that their jobs were being belittled by a woman.

Jackie suspected even another reason for their anger. The pilots, who ranged from well-trained patriotic fliers to "ham" pilots, were being paid good tax-free money to ferry bombers. Jackie, an amateur, would fly without pay. She was a threat to them.

Whatever their reasons, one pilot "leaked" to a Boston newspaper the story of Jackie's proposed flight, obviously hoping that advance publicity would force a cancellation. Others tried to block the State Department from issuing her a special visa into the war zone.

After heated arguments, a compromise was proposed. Jackie could serve as First Officer and would be allowed to pilot the bomber en route. Captain Grafton Carlisle, who had defended Jackie at the secret meeting and even volunteered to serve as her navigator, must be at the controls for all takeoffs and landings. The crew, other than Jackie, would be male. Jackie accepted the compromise.

The first leg of the flight was set for an early June morning in 1941. They would fly from Montreal directly to Gander, Newfoundland, where they would refuel for the flight across the ocean. Jackie, as First Officer, was required to inspect the plane before takeoff. She was startled to discover that the oxygen had been hooked up incorrectly, the emergency tank of antifreeze was empty, and certain equipment, including an essential oxygen wrench, was missing. It was late afternoon before the crew, Captain Carlisle in control, would take off. Once they were airborne, the captain disappeared from the cockpit and went below to navigate. Jackie took over the controls.

In Newfoundland the next morning Jackie faced another delay

when she checked out the plane. A window in the pilot's cabin was cracked, and the mysterious oxygen wrench again was missing. She suspected foul play from a mechanic when she spied a wrench in his pocket. Upon her demand and a dollar from her pocket, he grudgingly returned it. Jackie herself patched the window with adhesive tape.

At dusk the plane took off. Again, Captain Carlisle left the cockpit as soon as the craft was airborne. And Jackie Cochran on June 17, 1941, became the first woman to fly a bomber across the ocean.

In England, Jackie, now about thirty-one years old, made good use of her time while awaiting a return flight to the states. Much of it was spent with Pauline Gower, the woman in charge of English female pilots already flying for their country. Jackie studied their procedures, their living arrangements, and their places of work. On July 1 she returned to her New York apartment, aching and weary from sitting cramped on the floor of a B-24 bomber with hardly space enough to stretch her legs. "I will not get up before noon tomorrow for anyone," she declared, dropping into bed, "unless the president of the United States calls."

At nine the next morning President Franklin D. Roosevelt did call with an invitation to an early lunch at Crum Elbow, his elegant Hyde Park home about forty miles away. Jackie jerked outfits from her closet, dressed hurriedly, and, with the assistance of a police escort through traffic-tangled Manhattan streets and out into the countryside, made the luncheon engagement on time.

For two hours the president pumped Jackie for information on war-torn England through the eyes of a pilot. He showed particular interest in the role English women were playing in the war effort. "Women on this side of the ocean can do the same," Jackie insisted. Her comments were premature, however. The

United States was not yet at war and there still were plenty of male pilots available. Jackie wondered wearily if her arduous bomb flight had been made in vain.

At that moment Jackie did not know that within a few days she would be caught up in a dizzying whirlwind of activity that would drastically change her lifestyle. For the next three years she would be engaged in World War II (WWII). She would leave her cosmetic business to rock along on its own and during those years would spend fewer than ten nights in her own home.

Nor did she know at that moment that Floyd, too, would take up the war cry. Assuming a leave of absence from his business, he would accept an appointment from President Roosevelt as

Jackie relaxes with Floyd after her bomber flight in 1941.

director of the Office of Production Management for the federal government, a job for which he would be paid one dollar a year. Floyd would remain primarily in Washington, far from his beloved ranch and his handsome New York apartment. Worst of all, he would be separated from Jackie for big chunks of time and would have to content himself with daily wires, calls, or letters from his absent wife.

Jackie Cochran was going to war.

TEN

A few days after Jackie's Hyde Park visit, Mrs. Eleanor Roosevelt, wife of the president, summoned her to the White House. A firm believer in the ability and importance of women, she wanted to discuss with Jackie the role of women pilots in the military. Jackie, of course, was convincing in her enthusiasm.

A week later Jackie was again summoned to Washington, this time for a conference with General Arnold. The general delivered some news he suspected would elate Jackie. The British needed yet more women pilots. They had requested that Jackie recruit qualified female fliers from the United States and transport them to England to serve.

Jackie was dismayed. This was not the kind of service she had in mind. She wanted women actively flying side by side with men for the United States, not flying light planes for England. General Arnold, however, advised her to take the challenge. In England she could get experience for similar work in this country, and he would call her home when the time was right.

Jackie accepted. Any action was certainly better than staying home and knitting socks for soldiers.

The British first requested up to two-hundred women pilots. Jackie found the names of seven-hundred women pilots on file, but only seventy-five were what she termed qualified without additional intense training. She had no way of knowing how many of the seventy-five would be willing and able to leave their homes and jobs and move to England. So the British reduced the request to twenty-five for a start.

Jackie set out in her plane on a cross-country trek to personally interview and hand-pick most of her candidates. The rest she flew to New York for interviews. She insisted that all sections of the country be represented. Further, the fliers selected had to be of splendid character and a credit to the United States.

Intense medical examinations and security checks followed. Then the group was sent to Montreal for flight tests, after which they set out for England by ship. Jackie was to fly another bomber overseas and greet the women when they arrived in England. A typhoid shot, however, resulted in an abscess on her leg and a stay in a Montreal hospital, and the bomber flight was canceled.

Jackie instead pulled herself from bed and took a flight from New York, doctoring her draining wound with sulfa powder and fresh dressings and arriving just in time to hail her women pilots when they stepped on English soil in April 1942.

Jackie, under the honorary British title of Flight Captain, quickly discovered roadblocks when she proceeded to set up the operation. The first was a demand for new medical checks for all the women. Anxious to get on with the work at hand, Jackie felt the British government should accept the military examinations the women had undergone in the states. They refused.

"Then I'll be first," Jackie snapped.

"Then strip naked," the doctor thundered.

Jackie refused. In some ways she was prudish to an extreme, but this time she was defending the pilots under her command. Charging fully clad from the doctor's office, she took her complaint all the way to the top brass and won her case. Jackie, the officials discovered, was certainly no pushover. After that, other roadblocks were easier to clear.

Jackie became unpopular with some of the established British pilots, however, both male and female. They resented her title of Flight Captain and found her manner much too flamboyant for a war-torn country. To see her ride around in a fine car and wearing a mink coat rankled their egos. Some of the fliers complained that she stayed in the Savoy Hotel and kept a London flat, although she was based officially some distance away.

Jackie's supporters, however, remained loyal. They pointed out that she was serving without pay and that she maintained the flat in London as a rest facility for her off-duty American pilots. As to quarters in the Savoy Hotel, Jackie later stated that she was instead staying at the home of a British official and his wife, who had set aside a room for her use.

Jackie mothered and protected her fliers. They were women of courage and great dedication. They adjusted to whatever plane they were assigned to ferry, moving them from base to base or from factory to base in war-torn skies. Jackie doubted that they would ever get the credit they deserved.

Food was scarce throughout England, and Jackie was always on the lookout for proper rations. One day she found a supply of grits in a store. The English were passing it up for they knew nothing about grits. But Jackie knew all about this traditional southeastern United States staple and laid in a supply. When canned goods arrived from the states, she cooked suppers of grits and ham and dished them out generously for her fliers.

Even during intense bombings, Jackie moved freely around London when off duty. Death, she reasoned, would come when her own number was up. In the meantime she preferred taking her chances in the open instead of in a bomb shelter. How she admired the English people, living their lives from day to day while their country was being ravaged and gutted, their homes literally crumbling beneath them, and their stomachs constantly yearning for something more than wartime rations!

One night during a particularly heavy air raid, Jackie wrapped herself in a blanket and sat outside on the front steps. The London skies were filled with flashing lights, the atmosphere charged with piercing sirens. Windowpanes shattered around her, a house across the street was blown to pieces, and another one just a block away was a direct hit.

War indeed was real.

ELEVEN

In September 1942, Jackie was summoned home by General Arnold. Three years had passed since her first meeting with Mrs. Roosevelt, and the United States was now hard at war. The time had come, General Arnold said, to establish a military flying program for women here at home.

Jackie's two-year commitment to England was not yet completed, but she knew they would release her when the United States called. Rushing about making arrangements for a quick departure, she found her enthusiasm mounting. Her dream of a female flying corps now hovered within arm's reach.

Her excitement, however, was soon doused. Upon landing in New York she was handed a newspaper clipping announcing that Nancy Harkness Love had been appointed director of the new Women's Auxiliary Flying Service (WAFS), a group of women pilots under the U.S. Ferry Command. This arrangement was not at all what Jackie had proposed both to Mrs. Roosevelt and General Arnold, and she felt betrayed.

Although Jackie considered Nancy Love an excellent pilot, she differed with her in philosophy. Nancy's plan was to recruit women fliers who had five hundred hours in the air. This would be an elite group for sure, for few women had the privilege or money to garner so many flying hours. In fact, fewer than one hundred women in the entire country would qualify.

Jackie's plan was quite different. She wanted to throw the program open to all women fliers within a certain age category, select the most qualified, then put them through intense training just as though they were male Air Force Cadets.

With her dander up, Jackie raced to Washington. Clutching the news clipping in her hand, she stormed from office to office and, in her words, "made the fur fly." Eventually, however, she reluctantly compromised. Nancy's WAFS would ferry planes for the Air Transport Command and would train at a New Castle, Delaware, base. Jackie would organize the Women's Flying Training Detachment to train pilots to later fly with the WAFS. The Howard Hughes Field near Houston, Texas, was chosen for the base of operation.

JACKIE WITH PRESIDENT ROOSEVELT AT THE WHITE HOUSE IN 1943.

When word of Jackie's recruitment spread she was deluged with more than 25,000 enthusiastic applicants—secretaries, actresses, housewives, war widows, or women who simply wanted to do something for the war effort. Jackie flew around the countryside, again personally interviewing as many as possible. The candidates had to be between 21 and 34 years old, at least 62.5 inches tall, and have 200 hours' flying experience (this was later reduced to 35). In November the first class of 28 met in Houston, and Jackie was there to greet them. They had traveled cross-country at their own expense, had been issued no uniforms, and had to scout around the city to find their own room in a motel or private home. Whatever doubts these women had at the moment were soon erased by Jackie's enthusiasm. "You are badly needed," she assured them.

Dressed in men's trousers, dungarees, or overalls, the women assembled at dawn in high spirits. They clambered aboard army trucks and set out on an eleven-mile trip to the air field, singing every mile.

"You may think you're pretty hot pilots," the commanding officer snapped when they lined up to begin their training. "I'd advise you to forget it." They would start training all over again, he thundered, and this time it would be "the Army way."

The Army way meant dividing the long day between flight training and a curriculum of ground school studies so thorough that the women even learned how to take an engine apart and put it back together again. They bored into mathematics, physics, meteorology, and navigation. They spent endless hours flying fixed courses, landing, then repeating the routine until they were flying "the Army way." The planes they were assigned were either aging civilian crafts or basic trainers that had seen better days. Jackie called them "claptrap." After a work-weary day the women had to report for an hour of vigorous calisthenics before dinner, then climb aboard the truck for the return trip to Houston, still singing. For this they were paid $150 a month.

Jackie was unhappy with the makeshift arrangements. She wanted her fliers living on base rather than scattered around town, and she promptly set out to find a new home for them. In May 1943 she succeeded. Avenger Field at Sweetwater, Texas, became available and Jackie got permission to use it. Now the women slept in barracks, six to a room, and lived a highly regimented army life—reveille at dawn and a march in formation to breakfast, taps and lights-out sixteen hours later, and the time between spent at work, work, work. They stood roll call and barracks inspection just as male cadets did, marched in drills and parades, and couldn't leave base without a pass. Yet these women were civilians.

Jackie as usual began her own private war. She felt her fliers deserved military status with hospitalization, insurance, and death benefits. And she felt they deserved uniforms. Gradually the women had started wearing khaki trousers, white shirts, and khaki overseas caps, which they purchased with their own money. But Jackie demanded that Washington issue them their own uniforms. Displeased with the one the government eventually produced, she used her own money to have a uniform and beret designed at Bergdorf Goodman, a fashionable New York department store. She engaged a beautiful woman to model it, and demanded that this was the uniform she wanted even if the women had to buy it from their own pockets. She won her point, and the government picked up the tab.

Jackie set up strict rules of conduct for her fliers. She demanded that they always "act like ladies," that they always emerge from the cockpit with their hair combed, and that they obey curfews even on days off. She was so protective about

JACKIE IN HER WASP UNIFORM.

where they went and with whom that Avenger Field came to be called "Cochran's Convent."

Shortly after her move to the Sweetwater base, Jackie began a campaign to consolidate her program with the WAFS. On August 5, 1943, the two organizations became the Women's Airforce Service Pilots, or WASP, with Jackie as director and Nancy as staff executive for the ferrying division. Exercising her new authority, Jackie promptly assigned her fliers to jobs other than ferrying. She sent fifty WASPs to tow targets for student aircraft gunners at Camp Davis, North Carolina, a job male pilots both feared and detested. It required cruising at 10,000 feet with muslin targets trailing the plane so that student gunners on the ground could practice. The novice gunners often missed the targets and peppered the plane itself. Many a WASP

JACKIE AT THE WHEEL WITH SOME OF HER WASP FLIERS.

returned to base with holes in the plane's tail section and a fluttering heart under her uniform.

The success of these target-towers led to other dangerous assignments. WASPs took part in simulated gas attacks, performed smoke laying, and even did simulated low-level strafing while gun crews tracked them. To Jackie's delight, her fliers proved their courage time and again. And they proved something else—female biology and size do not prevent women from doing "men's work," even during wartime. One WASP, Betty Gillies, was so petite that she couldn't reach the rudder pedals. But this didn't stop her. She had wooden blocks fitted on the larger planes and continued flying.

The primary duty of the WASPs, however, was to ferry planes, and they did it well and quickly. Sometimes a WASP would ferry ten planes a day and stay right on schedule. Many commanding officers became so pleased with their work that they preferred WASPs over male pilots.

Of the 25,000 women who applied, 1,830 were accepted and 1,074 graduated—38 lost their lives. One of the casualties was Evelyn Sharp, who was thrown through the canopy of a P-38 as she crash-landed. Because she was a civilian she was not eligible for death benefits, a fact that weighed heavily on Jackie. Fellow pilots passed their berets and took up a collection to cover some of the cost. In all, WASPs delivered 12,650 planes, flew sixty million miles, and proved to the world that women indeed could serve their country.

But, Jackie lost a big battle that haunted her through the years. The bill to militarize the WASPs finally came to a vote and was denied by Congress on June 21, 1944. Shortly thereafter, on December 20, 1944, the WASP program was suddenly deactivated. Victory in Europe was now in sight, and male pilots were returning home to take over the jobs WASPs were performing. Jackie's fliers read the notice through tears. When victory, now only months away, did come, they wouldn't be around to celebrate. They'd be home looking for jobs. Few of them ever again would have a chance to enter a cockpit and they knew it.

This remarkable chapter of history gradually faded in memory, and today a large segment of the American public would be hard put to recall the story of the WASPs. But the WASPs themselves stayed in touch and met for reunions from time to time. At least one reunion was held at Jackie's ranch. Quietly but steadily they lobbied Congress for militarization. Finally just before midnight on November 4, 1977, designated "The Year of the WASP," Congress signed the bill ordering the militarization of the WASPs and granted them honorable discharges thirty-three years after they had been deactivated, and only nine months before Jackie's death.

A few months after the WASP was deactivated, Jackie received a telephone call telling her she would be awarded the Distinguished Service Medal (DSM). "What the devil is that?" she blurted into the phone. The caller told her that, except for the Medal of Honor, it was the highest honor possible and that she would be the first woman to receive it.

When Jackie was told that President Roosevelt would present the medal, her joy diminished. While she meant no disrespect to the president, she felt that General Arnold had made her war work possible, and she wanted him to make the presentation. "If he can't do it, then I don't want the medal," she declared.

General Arnold was seriously ill at the time, having just suffered a heart attack. After his recovery several months later, Jackie walked into his office in the Pentagon wearing her WASP uniform. "I thought you got the DSM," the general said, noting that she was not wearing the medal. "I'm waiting for you to give it to me," Jackie replied.

"You don't turn down the president!" he gasped.

"Well I did," Jackie retorted. "If you won't present it I'll just get it by mail."

Three mornings later in a large conference room at the Pentagon, an impressive assemblage of generals, admirals, and colonels in dress uniform watched as General Arnold made the formal presentation. Jackie stood tall and proud, blinking briskly to hide the tears in her eyes.

JACKIE RECEIVING THE DSM FROM GENERAL ARNOLD IN 1945.

TWELVE

Jackie's work with the WASPs was over, but she wasn't through with World War II. She still wanted to get to the Pacific Theater where the United States was battling Japan. She requested military jobs but they were slow coming through. Growing impatient, she volunteered her services as a reporter for *Liberty* magazine. Jackie was not a polished writer, but the editor knew the Odlums personally and had no doubt that Jackie would deliver interesting material. Jackie got the job, along with a priority rating that permitted her to travel into war areas.

General Arnold meanwhile issued Jackie military orders as a Special Consultant with certain duties to perform in the Pacific. Although she suspected he did this as a favor for her work during the war, it helped her gain military transportation as she hopscotched around the world.

Jackie hoboed from plane to plane and from island to island, grabbing whatever space was available in whatever craft was headed in the right direction. She managed to be in the Philippines when Japan surrendered and became the only woman permitted at the ceremony. Although other women reporters were barred, Jackie used her military status to gain admission. She also became the first American woman to land in Japan after the war.

From Tinian Island, which Jackie called a "speck in the Pacific," she wrote *Liberty* magazine that "baseball fever has engulfed the island" only two weeks after the war ended. With their last bomb run behind them, the servicemen set to work leveling cane fields and constructing a baseball diamond while awaiting their orders to go home. Former professional players had arrived from the states to stage exhibition games to entertain the war-weary soldiers, and Jackie interviewed them. But her article made it clear that "getting home was the predominant thought" on Tinian. "May they soon all be home . . . to participate in building a better world in which wars never happen again!" she wrote in the October 27, 1945, issue of *Liberty*.

JACKIE ON TINIAN ISLAND WITH BASEBALL PROFESSIONALS BIRDIE TEBBETTS, ENOS SLAUGHTER, AND JOE GORDON.

Jackie proceeded to Japan, where she discovered an official file on both Amelia Earhart and herself for reasons unknown. In China she had lunch in the country home of Madame Chiang Kai-shek, who presented her with the Chinese Air Wings as a salute for her war work and made arrangements for Jackie to be shown the finest silks available. Through Floyd's cousin, General Victor Odlum, an ambassador from Canada, she visited Mao Tse-tung, who kept postponing her departure until two hours had flown by. And in Persia (now Iran) she sipped tea with the Shah, Reza Pahlavi, before flying on to Europe. Wherever she went she was treated like royalty, a circumstance she could scarcely have foreseen as a child on Sawdust Road.

Of all the exceptional experiences Jackie enjoyed, the one that brought her the greatest joy was her visit with Pope Pius XII in Rome. Her fascination with the city was immediate. On the night before her scheduled audience with the pope, she donned warm clothes and a trenchcoat and walked the streets alone. The war had just ended, but the city still observed blackout regulations. No street lights were burning, and windowpanes were still draped in black. Jackie strolled by moonlight, enthralled by St. Peter's Cathedral, the Coliseum, the Forum, and returned to her hotel only a few hours before dawn and her scheduled audience with the pope.

At the Vatican she was moved from room to room awaiting her turn. In each room a little ceremony took place, heightening her anticipation. In the last room she was told that private audiences with the pope were lasting only two or three minutes that day. The pope would offer her a choice of a medal or a rosary blessed by him, and this would be her signal to leave. She must then depart immediately.

After entering the small, simple audience room, she knelt, received the blessing, and was stunned when the pope asked her to sit. He wanted to ask her impressions of China. He listened attentively as Jackie answered his questions, then rose and walked with her to the door, where he bade her farewell. As he turned away Jackie quickly stole a glance at her watch. Twenty-eight minutes with the pope! The memory of that meeting lifted her spirits "thousands of times" later.

The now-famous Nuremberg trials, where Hitler's officials would be tried for war atrocities, were set for November 1945. When Jackie arrived they had been in progress four days. Jackie watched the faces of the men on trial and could summon no sympathy. They deserved the sentences of hanging that were meted out, she said later. She visited the document room and saw signed orders by Hitler and his men approving the atrocities, and later she viewed in horror the prisons where thousands of Jews were gassed.

From Nuremberg she traveled to Berlin and was appalled to find women and children living in cold basements or gutted holes in the walls of the heavily bombed city. At night these people came out on the streets to scavenge for scraps of food left in the military garbage cans. Jackie asked a friend to drive her around the snow-crested streets while she handed out food. Just as she depleted her supply, she saw a woman pulling a child in a wagon, with four other small children tagging behind. Through her German driver she learned the woman's story. Her husband had disappeared during the war, whether captured or killed she did not know. She and her children were constantly hungry and she begged for food, but Jackie had given away her last morsel. A few blocks later Jackie suddenly remembered seeing food stored in the trunk of the car and she pleaded with her driver to take her back to find the woman. The driver argued that the search would be fruitless, for the streets now overflowed with people. In the dark they would all look alike. But luck was with them. They found the woman with her pitiful family, and filled their wagon with sugar, eggs, bread, cocoa, and a can of fruit juice. The woman's tears of joy froze on her cheeks in the cold Berlin air.

Jackie had one last burning desire before she left Germany. She wanted to see the bunkers of the Reichschancellery where Hitler is believed to have died. The bunkers, to her dismay, were guarded by Russians who persistently turned her group away. Finally she returned alone and bribed a guard with cigarettes and money. She found the bunkers to be a fabulous underground home, elegantly furnished and even air-conditioned.

When Jackie returned to the states she carried with her a gleaming gold doorknob from Hitler's bathroom, which she obtained in exchange for a pack of cigarettes. The keepsake served as a reminder that it would never again be used by the man who had created so much misery.

THIRTEEN

After the war Jackie resumed air racing and established new international and intercontinental records. In 1949 she was declared the outstanding woman pilot of the decade by the Harmon trophy committee, and in 1950 she set a new international speed record for propeller-driven airplanes when she piloted her P-51 around a 311-mile course at a little better than 447 miles per hour.

Floyd remained her most ardent admirer, on hand to greet her after each victory despite great difficulties in traveling. A few years after their marriage Floyd had developed a very painful and crippling arthritis and had to use a cane for walking. Through the years the arthritis would grow steadily worse and eventually confine him to a wheelchair. Always in good spirits, he suffered quietly and continued to conduct his business brilliantly, whether from a wheelchair or a bed.

Jackie loathed Floyd's pain and prayed almost constantly for his health. "If you get well and I am sick with arthritis I will assume my prayers have been answered and will not complain," she wrote him in 1949. At the time she was gravely ill herself in Vienna from one of her sudden onslaughts of abdominal problems. She was never able to remove her husband's pain, but she did fill his life with joy. He doted on her, their friends observed.

JACKIE RECEIVES THE HARMON TROPHY FROM PRESIDENT HARRY TRUMAN (THIRD FROM LEFT) IN 1950.

A hug or a kiss from Jackie produced a smile on his face and a glow that lasted all day.

After Jackie's 1950 victory in the P-51, she realized that racing propeller-driven planes was a thing of the past. Reluctantly she closed the door on this chapter of her life and devoted more time to her business. As Floyd predicted on the night they met, she did need an airplane. Now she was flying more than 90,000 miles a year on business alone.

When not traveling she spent time in her laboratory experimenting with new cosmetic products. Marilyn Monroe needed a special lip gloss to keep her mouth moist and glowing for the movie *Gentlemen Prefer Blondes*. Jackie produced it. Women in general needed moisture creams, so Jackie developed the highly successful "Flowing Velvet." She herself needed cosmetic travel

Jackie in her laboratory with two of her chemists.

items, so she designed "Perk Up," a cylinder only three and one-half inches long containing every cosmetic item needed for a short trip. In both 1953 and 1954 she was named American Business Woman of the Year by the Associated Press, and her name and photograph were splashed across leading newspapers and magazines.

Jackie's home base was split between the Odlums' twelve-room apartment in River House, 435 East 52nd Street in Manhattan, New York City, and the California ranch. Both were fascinating settings for a social life that included presidents, generals, royalty, movie stars, and, of course, famous pilots. The entrance hall of the River House apartment was a monument to aviation. The floor was laid in the design of a compass. Its walls were lined with photographs of airplanes and showcases of trophies that Jackie had won.

The ranch in California was a lush oasis in the desert. Tangerine and grapefruit trees clustered in thick groves along the driveway. Green grass, shade trees, and exotic shrubs transformed desert sand into picturesque landscapes. The Odlums kept a stable of fine Arabian horses, their own private golf course, tennis courts, and an Olympic-size swimming pool, which was warmed to ninety degrees to soothe Floyd's aching joints. Jackie and Floyd, telephones within reach, often conducted business by the pool. Each had a private secretary and a personal maid. They shared a telephone switchboard and operator.

The main house was furnished comfortably rather than lavishly and was managed by a team of servants. Guest houses dotted the landscape, and they were frequently occupied, for Jackie liked to be surrounded by people. Her favorite guests were other pilots, with whom she would sit up all night discussing flying. But all guests, whether a president or a pilot, succumbed to her

JACKIE IN THE ENTRANCE HALL OF HER RIVER HOUSE APART-
MENT.

wishes. She carted them off to the golf course or for an automobile tour of the ranch at her will, often driving at breakneck speed, and insisted that they drink and gamble after dinner if that's what she wanted to do. Her friends relished invitations to dinner. They never knew if they would be seated by a president or a movie star, or simply an unknown person. But they knew that the person would be interesting, for Jackie was drawn to people who did unusual or exciting things. Not all of her guests wanted to return, however. Some found her bossy and overbearing and they refused later invitations.

Although she wore ill-fitting pants and fatigues while flying or working around a plane, Jackie was vain about her appearance and loved to dress up. Even as early as the 1930s when her money was limited, she was noted for her trim, man-tailored silk suits. Many years later she would return from Paris with a new wardrobe of luxurious silks and handsome jewelry. In a burst of generosity, she ushered her closest friends into her bedroom and threw open the closet door. "Here, take this," she said, dealing out her designer clothes like a deck of cards. She'd even pay to have them altered to fit a friend.

Magazine articles called Jackie a "Golden Girl" and referred to her blonde hair, her porcelain complexion and flashing dark eyes. But Jackie spent hours in the sun playing golf or swimming, and her porcelain complexion became sun-damaged through the years.

In many of her personal habits Jackie's early life on Sawdust Road left its mark. As if to scrub away the memory of shacks with no soap or running water, she took several baths a day. Sometimes she spent hours dressing, shampooing and styling her hair. One time she even insisted that President Lyndon Johnson, telephoning from the White House, call her back later because she was busy washing her hair. He did.

Jackie was always drawn to young people. Wherever she went, even in foreign countries, she would single out youths and often, without fanfare, would "adopt" them by setting aside money for their care and education. She paid to educate dozens of boys and girls, personally replying to every letter she received from a young person, and devoting many hours to Camp Fire Girls. She was often asked to visit schools, to speak or to write for youths. She considered these invitations an honor and labored for hours, writing her scripts by hand before having them typed. Her primary message was to "toughen your mental muscles and get cracking in the right direction under your own power." In an article to the *San Diego Union* she challenged young people to "open up your power plants of energy, clean up your spark

JACKIE VISITS A SCHOOL IN NORTH HOLLYWOOD IN 1955.

plugs of ambition and pour in the fuel of work—and more work."

To the *New York Journal-American* she wrote that the first rule of beauty was to be feminine. Then she outlined five rules for skin care: cleanliness (including hair), moisturizers, proper makeup, protection from sun, and plenty of rest and exercise.

Although Jackie said she would be the last person in the world to write a book, in 1946 she began her autobiography. She wrote it for young people, she said. She wanted to assure them that they could succeed regardless of humble beginnings. Realizing how difficult it was for Jackie to put words onto paper, Floyd constantly encourged her. "Write, Jackie," he reminded her whenever she had a spare moment. So Jackie wrote in the evenings when she and Floyd were home alone. The book, *The Stars at Noon*, was published by Little, Brown and Company in 1953.

FOURTEEN

"That man will be president of the United States one day," Jackie said to the gentleman sitting next to her at a dinner in 1946. The man she referred to was General Dwight D. (Ike) Eisenhower. General Eisenhower had served as Supreme Commander of the Allied Forces in Europe during WWII and had become the nation's number one hero. Later that same evening Jackie found herself seated next to the famous general.

"Why don't you run for president?" she asked in her customary forthright manner. The general was slightly amused. He was still greatly involved in the military and had not given politics even one thought.

The groundswell had begun, however, and five years later the general's popularity still soared. The Republican party was searching for a likely presidential candidate. General Eisenhower then was living in France as head of the North Atlantic Treaty Organization (NATO). Each time the subject of the presidency was mentioned, he countered with, "If I get a clear-cut call from the American people, I'll give it consideration." So a group of his supporters set out to provide a "clear-cut call," and Jackie was selected to play a role.

Jackie was asked to organize a rally of "people for Ike" at Madison Square Garden in New York City. "Why me?" she asked. "Because we think you'll do a good job," came the reply. She did.

On the evening of the rally in February 1952, more than 21,000 exuberant Ike supporters converged on New York from all parts of the country. Even more lined the streets outside. "Holler with your dollar," they yelled. The rally lasted till five o'clock in the morning, and a great deal of it had been captured on film as the "clear-cut call" to Ike.

The film was developed overnight. The next morning Jackie collected the footage and caught a flight to Paris. She was to be allotted a half hour in the general's office. "I believe I am carrying a message of utmost importance from the common people of our country," she said, "and I have only thirty minutes." Then she asked that she not be interrupted. Words tumbled from her lips as her allotted time sped by. At the end Ike refused to rush her out the door and instead made arrangements to be shown a few minutes of the film. Ten minutes later he halted the showing and invited Jackie to his home so his associates and his wife, Mamie, could see the footage. Before the evening was over Eisenhower was talking about honor and duty and his debt to his country. With tears in his eyes, he sent Jackie back to the states with requests that certain people get in touch with him. A week later Ike consented to run.

Zigzagging back and forth across the country, Jackie threw herself into the campaign with the same vigor with which she approached air racing. She made speeches, raised money, and organized rallies. Floyd meanwhile worked behind the scenes. The slogan, "I Like Ike," was coined in the Odlums' New York apartment. On election day Jackie and Floyd returned to their ranch to await the results on a new television set. These were the early days of television, however, and the set refused to work, so they heard the announcement by radio. Adlai Stevenson had conceded, and Ike was declared winner by an overwhelming majority. Jackie and Floyd went outside and shouted joyously at the stars.

The Odlum-Eisenhower friendship continued through the years, a genuine caring relationship far removed from politics and power. General and Mrs. Eisenhower were frequent visitors to the ranch, and Ike lived in one of their guest cottages while he wrote his memoirs. Jackie was so protective of his privacy that she appeared at his cottage by invitation only. Further, she had a personal switchboard installed so his calls could bypass the business switchboard that she and Floyd used.

Inspired by President Eisenhower and still fervently patriotic, Jackie decided in 1955 to run for Congress from her California district. The president publicly endorsed her and telephoned to

JACKIE AND FLOYD WITH FORMER PRESIDENT EISENHOWER IN 1966.

say he was looking forward to having her nearby in Washington. Floyd, however, privately opposed her candidacy, reminding her that she lacked the tact to be a successful politician. He was right. Although she campaigned vigorously by airplane, even visited workers in the fields, her flamboyant manner was misunderstood. She was soundly defeated.

The defeat devastated Jackie and she slumped into deep depression. "Actually I crawled into a corner and licked my wounds," she said later, and she never again entered politics.

FIFTEEN

Floyd once said that Jackie knew no fear. Jackie herself said she conquered fear one night on Sawdust Road when she was still a child. It was already dark as she said goodbye to her friends and set out for home. Her playmates called after her, taunting her with tales of a ghost that was sure to grab her when she passed the cemetery. "You'll be so scared you'll come running back," they teased. Sure enough, as she started across a wooden walkway that ran through the graveyard, a live "ghost" with arms and legs did rise to meet her. Jackie had to choose between retreating to her jeering playmates or tackling the ghost head on. She decided to tackle. Screaming, she dashed forward and ran headlong into the creature, which turned out to be a frightened calf whose hind legs were trapped in a broken board. From then on Jackie tried to think of fears as only scared calves whose hind legs were trapped.

Years later, after she became a pilot, Jackie found that she did get emotionally charged before a race, but she refused to call the emotion fear. People told her she cried out in her sleep. Sometimes she had chills and shakes, but she never let them show. At the starting line she always waved nonchalantly before taking off. Spectators never saw her deep concern over weather conditions, or whether or not her plane, overloaded with extra fuel, would even get off the ground. At the finish line she combed her hair and applied fresh lipstick before alighting, then smiled engagingly before the camera and microphone. Never would the onlookers guess that Jackie had lost six pounds during the race, a considerable drop for her trim figure. Nor would they realize that she at times descended from great heights with only minutes of gasoline left in the tank. One time, Jackie's plane broke in two as she landed, and Jackie was covered with oil and gasoline that easily could have ignited. Twenty minutes later, she boarded a commercial airliner to New York to keep a dinner date with Floyd. Even after Jackie crash-landed in 1939, the result of a defective landing gear, she acknowledged no fear. She had a theory about crash landings, she explained. As long as the pilot walked away from the plane, the landing was only "an incident."

JACKIE'S PLANE CRASHED WHILE LANDING DUE TO DEFECTIVE LANDING GEAR, 1939.

But in the post-WWII years a fear grew larger in Jackie's mind than the graveyard calf. This time she let it show. Since 1932 Jackie had been at the center of aviation, but the end of the war heralded a new era in the air. The propeller-driven planes that Jackie had flown to exhilarating heights and speed were now being replaced. Sleek supersonic jets, the most profound development since the Wright brothers' plane, ribboned the sky with white vapor trails. New records were being set almost daily but they were all set by men. All jets at the time belonged to the military and no woman had been cleared for military flying—not even Jacqueline Cochran, a pilot and Lieutenant Colonel in the Air Force Reserve and one of the best fliers in the world.

Was the jet age passing her by?

From the sidelines Jackie envied those bright, young pilots selected for jet training. How she longed to join them! The one she admired the most was Captain Charles (Chuck) Yeager (he has since become a general). Yeager, only twenty-four years old and already distinguished as a war ace, was in the forefront of jet aviation and in 1946 had become the first man to break the sound barrier. Now he was test-piloting the X-1 research rocket, a privilege for which Jackie probably would have sacrificed her lottery-ticket doll.

The two found themselves in the same room during a 1947 official conference in Washington. "Great job," Jackie said, pumping Yeager's hand. "We're all proud of you." Then she invited him to lunch.

Yeager had never met Jackie before and, even more significant, didn't seem to know much about her. As they entered the posh restaurant he watched in amazement the drama she incited. The owner, bowing low, heralded her like a queen. Waiters almost danced around her, then scurried to do her bidding. Over sparkling silver and gleaming tablecloths, the two pilots' conversation immediately went airborne. They both loved flying, they both were competitive, and both were among the world's greatest pilots. Jackie spoke of her eagerness to fly jets and told Yeager how she had been knocking on doors trying to gain permission. "If I were a man I would have been a war ace like you," she said. "Then generals would be pounding on my door instead of the other way around." Yeager meanwhile answered her volley of questions about jet flying.

"Let's stay in touch," Jackie said in parting.

The friendship that began that day endured until Jackie's death and expanded to include their families. Jackie considered Yeager the world's best pilot and lived vicariously through his repeated feats of courage and daring. Yeager meanwhile learned to value Jackie's aviation skills and called her not only a good friend but a "damn good pilot."

Yeager and his wife became close friends, and the Odlum-Cochran ranch became second home to the couple and their children. Even so, Yeager resented Jackie's bossiness, even down to telling him what tie to wear. And at first his wife Glennis resented the way Jackie took over their lives and suspected she was using Yeager to further her own career. But the years that followed proved Jackie's friendship true. She saw them through sickness and health, and bullied generals and chiefs of staff until Yeager finally was awarded a Congressional Medal of Honor.

But that Washington luncheon set in motion something more immediate. For years Jackie has pursued people in power, requesting the privilege of testing jets. She wrote letters, sent telegrams, made long-distance calls, and flew to Washington to plead her case. Finally she applied to airplane manufacturers for an assignment as flight consultant and test pilot. Floyd at the time was president of Canadair, a Canadian firm building the sleek and powerful F-86 Sabre-jet. Even so, two years passed before, in 1953, Jackie was hired as a civilian employee to run a number of routine tests at Edwards Air Force Base near Jackie's ranch. Her request, which required unraveling yards of government red tape to permit her to use an air base, eventually was granted. Jackie promptly asked Yeager to be her mentor, swearing him to secrecy. If news were to leak that a civilian, and a woman at that, would be using a military base, the tests probably would be canceled.

The young Chuck Yeager put Jackie, now about forty-three years old, through grueling paces, testing her first in the T-33 jet trainer and later in the F-86. Flying an Air Force F-86 himself, he instructed her by radio and flew so close he could watch her hands on the controls. Finally he signaled her to climb

JACKIE WITH HER MENTOR, CHUCK YEAGER.

to 45,000 feet, higher than they had flown on previous days, and Jackie knew the great hour was at hand.

In the early days of jet aviation it was necessary to put the plane into a steep dive to gain enough speed to reach Mach 1, the speed of sound. Mach 1, however, can vary with fluctuations of temperature and the distance above sea level. The variation can run from 680 miles per hour in very cold climates to almost 800 in hot temperatures. In the heat of the desert, Jackie's speed would be close to the top limit. As the plane dives, it first catches up with the waves radiating from its engines. Later, if the speed is great enough, it breaks through the waves as though they were an invisible wall. The breakthrough sets off intense vibrations inside the plane and creates a sonic boom that can be heard far below. It's a moment that demands intense concentration and excellent flying skills, and Jackie was ready for it. No lurking fear taunted her, no memory of her early graveyard encounter with a ghost. Her nerves were taut, her senses alert, her hands ready.

The climb to 45,000 feet seemed to take forever. As they flew over her ranch, Jackie left in her wake a vapor trail that signaled Floyd, waiting below in his wheelchair, that today was the day. At last, close to the Mexican border, Jackie got the signal from Chuck to nose dive. There, at the top of the world, she began her split "S" curve to an almost vertical dive, the throttle at full power. Jackie stole glances at the meter and radioed her reading to Yeager: "Mach .97, Mach .98, Mach .99." Only .02 faster and she'd be flying at the speed of sound!

Hanging face down, she felt blood surging into her head with such force she feared she would pass out. Pain raced across her abdomen; her legs throbbed. "Why, oh why, didn't I wear a 'G' suit?" Jackie berated herself. But she knew the answer. She had been provided a "G" suit but she learned that "oldsters" at

Edwards no longer bothered to wear them. Jackie had refused it.

"Tell me what you're feeling," Yeager radioed.

"Shock waves look like rain," Jackie replied inanely. But she was feeling much more, something like being inside an explosion. Suddenly there was silence as the high-pitched whine of her plane fell far behind, and a certain "knowing" washed over her. She had reached a pinnacle in her life. Nothing else would surpass the thrill of it for as long as she lived.

Jacqueline Cochran was flying faster than the speed of sound.

SIXTEEN

Back on the ground from her first supersonic flight, Jackie was greeted with hugs and kisses and rounds of congratulations. Then through the din she heard a disturbing announcement. "The control tower didn't catch it when you broke the barrier," someone said. "Do you want to break it again for the record?"

"Sure," Jackie replied.

"When?" the voice asked.

"Right now," Jackie fired back.

An hour later Jackie was back in the sky, flying so high that she actually saw the stars at noon. This time her feat was officially recorded:

May 18, 1953—Jacqueline Cochran became the first woman to break the sound barrier.

Two weeks later Jackie and Yeager ascended to almost 50,000 feet to fly a supersonic duet for *Life* magazine and Paramount Pictures, the fastest woman and the fastest man in the world flying separate planes wing tip to wing tip through the sound barrier. The feat was spectacular, but sonic booms played a trick on them. Sound waves dashed the camera and destroyed the film footage that today would be a treasure.

Jackie said that breaking the sound barrier was both a spiritual and an emotional experience. She felt a great humility and a trust in a divine order. But it had its price. She had spent years making it possible, had flown at least 10,000 miles back and forth across the country and into Canada trying to get clearance, she had spent weeks in grueling study and testing, and the flights landed her in the hospital to repair abdominal lesions. Anxious to get back in the air, she recovered rapidly.

Over the next few weeks Jackie canceled her plans to attend Queen Elizabeth's coronation and ran the long-awaited speed tests for Canadair. The closed courses were marked by pylons, with an official judge and a timer at each to clock her with electronic devices. Observation planes flew overhead. In order for cameras to record the events, the flights took place only several hundred feet above ground. If anything went wrong it would be almost impossible for Jackie to escape. Insurance for each flight was set at $10,000 for the plane alone, an astounding sum at the time. Statistically Jackie figured her chance of mishap was 50,000 times greater than in a routine flight. She measured the risks carefully, but she never dwelled on dangers. Getting on with the challenge was much more satisfying. And she was ready.

Yeager was officially appointed to observe her from a nearby chase plane, a tradition when testing experimental aircraft. In order to gain maximum speed they selected only the hottest days when the temperature was soaring. But boiling temperatures create turbulence. On one flight Jackie's plane vibrated so severely that one of her main tanks sprang a leak, sending fuel gushing from the wing and the side of her fuselage. At any moment the plane could explode. Jackie, of course, was not able to see the leak. Not wanting to alarm her, Yeager teased her with a radio message. "I thought you were a big girl," he said, "but you've got a wet bottom." He ordered her to "pull the damn airplane up, stop it, cock it, and pull it down on a dry lake bed." Then, unknown to Jackie, he radioed the tower to rush fire trucks to the scene. Jackie followed his order, although it meant a high-speed landing and a long roll. When her wheels touched ground Yeager ordered her to cut off all switches and jump free of the plane—fast!

Removing her oxygen mask, Jackie smelled gasoline and understood there would be no time to wait for a ladder. She scurried onto the wing and prepared to jump. Eyeing the hard lake-bed surface, she realized the long drop could break her legs. "Get over here, boy, and break my fall," she ordered a sergeant standing nearby. "No way, ma'am," the sergeant replied, eyeing the hot plane and the draining fuel. "Goddamn," Jackie yelled. She'd have to jump and take her chances.

Yeager's plane thundered to a halt. In one swift motion he jumped to the ground and raced to Jackie's side just as she lept from the Sabre-jet. He broke her fall.

During those late spring days in the California desert, Jackie Cochran spent only six hours flying a jet and chalked up only thirteen takeoffs and landings. Yet she set three world speed records and dived three times past the sound barrier, a remarkable achievement for a newcomer to the jet age.

For the next few years there were no jets available for Jackie to fly, but she was itching for new challenges. Eventually she persuaded Northrop, an airplane manufacturer, to hire her as a company pilot. Northrop leased one of their T-38s back from the Air Force and put Jackie in the cockpit. Again Chuck Yeager was her mentor as she, now in her fifties, set eight major speed records in 1961.

During this period she received her fourteenth Harmon trophy, this one presented by President John Kennedy, became the first woman to fly a jet across the Atlantic, and was elected president of the Federation Aeronautique Internationale, a prestigious organization consisting of 58 member nations with a home base in Paris. She was the first woman to serve as its president, a staggering honor in itself, and was reelected to serve a second term. To attend the convention in Moscow, Jackie flew her own twin-engined Lockheed Lodestar, a gift from Floyd. Chuck Yeager served as co-pilot, and in the cabin were Jackie's private secretary, maid, hairdresser, and personal interpretor.

When John Glenn orbited the earth in a spaceship on February 20, 1962, Jackie sat glued to her television set. Outer space was the new frontier and for years she had longed to conquer it.

Even before the Glenn orbit, Jackie had become involved in the space program. She was serving as a consultant to a National Air and Space Administration (NASA) official, James Webb, and both she and Floyd had put up seed money to start the first space medical research program.

At first the astronaut program was open to both men and women but it required experience as a jet test pilot or advanced engineering skill, both of which eliminated women. Except for Jackie, no woman had had an opportunity to qualify as a jet test pilot, and engineering schools at the time were not even admitting women. Yet Jackie was convinced that women, although physically smaller, would be excellent astronauts.

Jackie herself was too old to enter the program, so she set out to make it possible for other women to serve. She and her friend, Dr. Randy Lovelace, wanted to prove that women were as physically and emotionally capable as men to fly in space. They called in twenty of the most qualified women pilots and put them through the same medical tests that the men were required to take. Jackie paid the bills and Dr. Lovelace directed the testing. Twelve women passed. The women were then to proceed to Pensacola, Florida, for further checks in a Navy medical laboratory. And at that moment NASA squashed the women's astronaut program.

After the moon shot Jackie received a letter from NASA announcing that a small piece of the moon had been dedicated in her name.

Although Jackie was too old for the astronaut program, she continued making marks in the sky. In 1963 she signed on as a company pilot with Lockheed, manufacturer of the world's fastest planes. But she wasn't exactly greeted with cheers. The hundred or more pilots on staff, all young, grumbled and scoffed at the "old dame" trying to do their jobs.

But Jackie fell in love with the whole bunch. They were her type—pilots and daredevils. She rented a nearby room with kitchen privileges and every day she fried chicken, piled it high

JACKIE FLIES A WWII FIGHTER PLANE.

in picnic baskets, and lugged the baskets to the airfield. But it wasn't her chicken that won those pilots over. They watched in amazement as Jackie set two speed records in a Lockheed F-104 Starfighter, a Mach 2 plane that frightened many pilots. The next year, 1964, she broke three more records, two of which were improvements on international records she had already established.

By then no pilot dared even whisper of Jackie Cochran as an "old dame."

SEVENTEEN

During the 1960s Jackie sold her cosmetic business for a tidy sum and the Odlums now spent most of their time at the California ranch. Their days were seldom idle. Jackie spent several hours every morning on the telephone or with her secretary. Floyd, with swimming tubes strapped to his arms to keep him afloat, conducted business from their heated swimming pool, the only source of relief for his aching joints. Dignitaries and executives swarmed in and out of their ranch as if it were a Wall Street office.

Jackie continued to quell her restless nature with long, exciting trips in her Lodestar, some of them with Chuck Yeager. Once she and Floyd flew to Spain where they were guests of General Franco.

Jackie never stopped working in the interest of aviation. She served tirelessly on boards and committees, including a presidential task force on aerial hijacking. And honors continued to pile up. In 1969 she was awarded the Distinguished Flying Cross by the U.S. Air Force. In 1971 she became the first living woman to be enshrined in the Aviation Hall of Fame in Dayton, Ohio.

Jackie never thought of herself as healthy. In addition to her abdominal problems, she had lost two pregnancies to miscarriages, which broke her heart for both she and Floyd wanted children. But she never thought of herself as over age twenty-five and was dismayed when she found that she was growing older and her health was declining. For years she concealed her problems from Floyd, aware that her suffering was nothing compared to his, but the time arrived when she could no longer keep it secret. She began blacking out. She could be holding a drink in her hand, carrying on a conversation, or simply combing her hair when the blackouts hit and she'd fall to the floor. They lasted only moments, and Jackie immediately resumed whatever she was doing. But the blackouts signaled a pressing problem. Jackie's heart was wearing out.

At nine o'clock one morning in 1971 Jackie's friend and ranch business manager, Aldine Tarter, rushed into the bedroom to wake Floyd, who was sleeping late. "Jackie is having seizures," she told him. "It's bad."

The spells were occurring regularly, but Jackie was unfazed. Between blackouts she helped Floyd and Aldine make plans for her to go to a hospital some distance away. The doctor advised against a flight for fear Jackie's heart could not stand the altitude. By land the trip would take twelve to fourteen hours. They made quick arrangements for two men on the ranch to prepare a station wagon with a bed in the back. The men and the station wagon were ready within the hour. But Jackie wasn't.

Between blackouts Jackie ordered that grapefruits and dates be picked and stowed atop the wagon as gifts for every doctor and nurse in the hospital. She packed suitcases to overflowing and had them stashed in the car. She bathed and dressed.

Then Aldine smelled the aroma of Jackie's famous fried chicken wafting through the house and found her friend standing over a frying pan. "We'll need it to eat along the way," Jackie explained innocently.

Then Jackie made one final arrangement. She asked Aldine to stay with Floyd to keep him from worrying.

"Oh, Jackie, don't die and leave me," Floyd said as he bade her goodbye.

Jackie returned with a pacemaker and the reality that she could never fly again. At first she couldn't look at the sky without crying. She walked outdoors at night and studied the moon and stars, which now seemed so far removed. But her self-pity was short lived. She bought a motor home and traveled the country the way she used to fly the sky—fast and often. She charged around the ranch on a three-wheeled bicycle, gathering fruits and vegetables, playing golf and continuing her work and play with her customary enthusiasm. And only a few months after

JACKIE DISCUSSING HIJACKING PROBLEMS WITH TWA CAPTAIN ARLIE NIXON, UNITED NATIONS AMBASSADOR GEORGE BUSH, AND UAL CAPTAIN JOHN KENT IN 1971.

her pacemaker was installed, she threw a party for a hundred people for Floyd's eightieth birthday.

Rewards still came to Jackie. In 1975, when she was about age sixty-five she was invited to donate her private papers to the Dwight D. Eisenhower Library in Abilene, Kansas. That same year she became the first woman to be honored by the U.S. Air Force Academy in Colorado Springs, Colorado. Being with the young, adoring cadets filled her with joy, and when they presented her with an official Air Force sword she nearly burst with pride.

Jackie and Floyd eventually sold the ranch to a developer and moved across the road to a large but more modest home. Again Jackie was heartbroken. The ranch and its lush beauty were an extension of Jackie. To let go of still another part of herself was devastating.

And within a short time Jackie had to give up another extension of herself. On June 18, 1976, Floyd died in Jackie's arms.

Happiness drained from Jackie's life. Despite her independence, Floyd had been the center of her existence. Now she felt unfocused.

Jackie's health plummeted. Her kidneys and her heart both failing, she became so swollen that she had to sit up at night to breathe. To be earth-bound to a frail body demanded more than she was able to give. At times she was so ill-tempered that friends hesitated to visit.

Jackie spoke of death and made arrangements for her funeral. It was to be simple, she insisted. Father Charles M. Depiere would conduct the service, and only a few of her closest friends would attend. She wanted no crowds to observe her departure the way they had gathered for her races. The one she wanted most of all, Floyd, certainly would not be sitting in his wheelchair wishing her off.

Although her friends suspected she was only teasing, Jackie demanded that her Air Force sword be buried with her. In case she "didn't go to heaven but went to the other place," she explained, she would use it to fight her way out. In the end she changed her mind and returned the sword to the Air Force Academy, where it remains today on display.

On August 9, 1980, Jacqueline Cochran died. Two days, later, under a sun-drenched sky just right for flying, she was laid to rest in a simple pine coffin topped with yellow roses. Inside the coffin lay her lottery-ticket doll.

Overhead, vapor trails from distant jets drifted slowly across the sky, scattered, and eventually disappeared in the hot desert air.

Appendix

Important Events in Jacqueline Cochran's Career

Even in death Jacqueline Cochran continues to hold more international speed, distance, and altitude records than any other pilot, male or female, dead or alive. The following are only highlights of a career that spanned more than three decades.

1932—Earns pilot's license.

1934—Enters her first air race: London to Australia

1935—Establishes Jacqueline Cochran Cosmetics. Enters first Bendix race.

1936—Marries Floyd B. Odlum on May 11.

1937—Wins first place in women's division of Bendix, third place overall. Becomes first woman to make blind landing. Wins her first of fifteen Harmon trophies as the outstanding woman pilot in the world.

1938—Wins first place in Bendix.

1939—Establishes a women's national altitude record. Wins New York to Miami air race.

1940—Breaks 2,000 kilometer international speed record.

1941—Becomes first woman to pilot a bomber across the ocean. Organizes twenty-five women to fly for Great Britain during WWII.

1942—Appointed director of women's flying training for the United States.

1943—Appointed to staff of U.S. Army Air Forces and director of Women's Airforce Service Pilots (WASP).

1945—Receives U.S. Distinguished Service Medal.

1953—Becomes first woman pilot to break the sound barrier.

1957—Becomes the only woman to receive the Air Force Association Award for distinguished civilian service.

1958–61—Becomes the only woman to be elected, and subsequently reelected, President of the Federation Aeronautique Internationale.

1962—Becomes first woman to fly a jet across the ocean.

1962–64—Establishes sixty-nine intercity and straight-line distance jet records. Sets nine international speed, distance, and altitude jet records. During this time she sets and resets a number of other jet records.

1969—Awarded Distinguished Flying Cross by U.S. Air Force.

1970—Presented Legion of Merit by U.S. Air Force.

1971—Becomes the first living woman to be enshrined in the Aviation Hall of Fame in Dayton, Ohio.

1975—Becomes the first woman to be honored at the U.S. Air Force Academy, Colorado Springs, Colorado, with a permanent display of her memorabilia. Her private papers become a permanent collection at the Dwight D. Eisenhower Library, Abilene, Kansas.

1980—Jacqueline Cochran dies at home on August 9. On November 6 a memorial service is held at the U.S. Air Force Academy.

Other Sources of Information on Jacqueline Cochran

The Smithsonian Book of Flight For Young People, by Walter J. Boyne. New York: Macmillan Publishing Company, 1988.

The Story of Flight, by John Lewellen and Irwin Shapiro. New York: Golden Press, 1959.

Women in Aeronautics, by Charles Paul May. New York: Thomas Nelson & Sons, 1962.

Women of the Air, by Judy Lomax. New York: Dodd, Mead & Co., 1987.

Yeager, by Chuck Yeager and Leo Janos. New York: Bantam Books, 1985.

Jackie Cochran, by Jacqueline Cochran and Maryann Bucknum Brinley. New York: Bantam Books, 1987.

Those Wonderful Women in Their Flying Machines, by Sally Van Wagenen Keil. New York: Rawson, Wade Publishers, Inc., 1979.

The Stars at Noon, by Jacqueline Cochran. Boston: Little, Brown and Company, 1954.

Women Aloft, by Valerie Moolman. Alexandria, VA.: Time-Life Books, 1981.

Jacqueline Cochran Exhibits

National Air and Space Museum, Smithsonian Institution, Washington, D.C.

U.S. Air Force Academy, Arnold Hall, Colorado Springs, Colorado.

International Women's Air and Space Museum, Centreville, Ohio.

Air Force Museum, Dayton, Ohio.

San Diego Aerospace Museum and International Hall of Fame, San Diego, California.

Jacqueline Cochran's oral history is contained at Columbia University, New York City, and her private papers are contained at the Dwight D. Eisenhower Library, Abilene, Kansas.

INDEX

AP-7 airplane, 46, 48
Air Transport Auxiliary (ATA),
    British, 51–53
Air Transport Command, 62
American Business Woman of the
    Year, Associated Press
1953 award, 78
1954 award, 78
Antoine, 26
Antoine's Salon
    in Miami Beach, 26, 28–29
    at Saks Fifth Avenue, 26, 29,
    43–44
Arnold, H. H. ("Hap"), 51, 52,
    57, 61, 70
    Distinguished Service Medal
    presented to Jackie by, 68–69
Associated Press, 78
Avenger Field (Sweetwater, Texas),
    64, 66
Aviation Hall of Fame, 100

B-24 bomber, 54
Beaverbrook, Lord William Max-
    well Aitken, 51–52
Bendix, Vincent, 48

Bendix Race from Los Angeles,
    California, to Cleveland,
    Ohio
1935 race, 37–41, 44
1938 race, 48–49
Bennett Field, Floyd (Long Island,
    N.Y.), 46
Bergdorf Goodman, 64
Bostwick, Miss, 9–12, 14, 18, 22,
    24

California, Jackie and Floyd's ranch
    in. See Cochran-Odlum Ranch
Camp Davis (North Carolina), 66
Camp Fire Girls, 81
Canadair, 90–91, 95
Carlisle, Grafton, 53, 54
Charles of the Ritz, 26
Chiang Kai-shek, Madame, 72
Chinese Air Wings, 72
Civil Aeronatics Administration, 39
Clifford Burke Harmon Trophy,
    49, 75, 96
Cochran, Jacqueline (Jackie)
    air racing career of, 32–41, 44,
    46, 48–49, 75, 76, 87–88

Cochran, Jacqueline (Jackie) (*cont'd*)
Air Transport Auxiliary (ATA)
and, 51–53
airline hostess jobs of, 32
autobiography of, 82
awards won by, 49, 68–69, 72,
78, 96, 100
beauty shop jobs of, 19–22, 24–
26, 28, 43–44
commercial pilot's license earned
by, 32
congressional candidacy of, 85–
86
cooking and, 15, 19
cosmetic business of, 37, 43–44,
76, 78, 100
death of, 68, 90, 103–4
determination of, 2, 14, 39
early life of, 1–3, 5–25, 72, 80,
87
education of, 9–12, 24–25
Eisenhower Library, private
papers at, 103
Eisenhower's 1952 presidential
campaign and, 83–85
end of her flying career, 102
fear and, 87–89
female pilots, status of, 32, 33,
37–38, 41, 44, 48, 51–55,
57–59, 61–64, 66–68, 70,
89–91, 97–99
flight training of, 30–32, 89–96
foster family of, 1–3, 5–7, 13,
15–20, 26
health of, 8, 50, 58, 75, 95,
100–103

honors bestowed upon, 96–97,
100, 103, 104
jet training of, 89–96
as *Liberty* magazine reporter,
70–74
Lockheed and, 98–99
marriage of. *See* Odlum, Floyd
B.
NASA and, 97–98
nursing training of, 23–24
orphanage established by, 43
pilot's license earned by, 30
real family roots traced by, 42
records achieved by, 46, 49, 54,
70, 75, 94–96, 99
religion and, 9
space medical research, support
for, 97
Stars at Noon, The (autobiography), 82
textile mill job of, 17–19
U.S. Air Force Reserve and, 89
Women's Airforce Service Pilots
(WASP) and, 66–68, 70
Women's Flying Training Detachment and, 62–64, 66
World War II and, 50–64, 66–
74
young people, message to, 81–82
Cochran Cosmetic Company,
Jacqueline
"Flowing Velvet," 76
founding of, 37
"Perk Up," 78
Rockefeller Center, move to, 43–
44
sale of, 100

Cochran-Odlum Ranch, 44, 56, 68, 84–85, 90, 91, 100, 101
description of, 78, 80
purchase of, 43
sale of, 103
Columbus, Georgia, Jackie's life in, 16–19
Congressional Medal of Honor, 90
Connecticut, Jackie and Floyd's estate in, 43
Curtiss Wright, 36

Depiere, Charles M., 103
Distinguished Flying Cross, U.S. Air Force, 100
Distinguished Service Medal (DSM), 68–69
Dwight D. Eisenhower Library, 103

Earhart, Amelia, 41, 72
final flight of, 44, 46
Jackie's friendship with, 38, 39, 44, 46
Edwards Air Force Base (California), 91, 93
Eisenhower, Dwight D. ("Ike")
Jackie's congressional candidacy endorsed by, 85–86
Jackie's support for 1952 presidential campaign of, 83–85
Eisenhower, Mamie, 84, 85
Eisenhower Library, Dwight D., 103
Elizabeth II, queen of England, 95

F-86 Sabre-jet, 91
F-104 Starfighter, 99
Fairchild airplane, 31
Father, Jackie's foster, 1, 3, 7, 9, 16
Federation Aeronautique Internationale, 96–97
Florida sawmill towns, Jackie's life in, 3, 5–16, 23–24, 72, 80, 87
"Flowing Velvet," 76
Floyd Bennett Field (Long Island, N.Y.), 46
Franco, Francisco, 100
Friendship (plane), 44

Gamma airplane, 37, 38, 40–41
Gee Bee airplane, 33–36
Gentlemen Prefer Blondes, 76
Gillies, Betty, 67
Glenn, John, 97
Gower, Pauline, 54
Granville Brothers airplanes, 33
Gypsy engine, 31

Harmon Trophy, Clifford Burke, 49, 75, 96
Henry (foster brother), 3
Hitler, Adolf, 50, 73, 74
Howard Hughes Field (Houston, Texas), 62–63
Hughes, Howard, 46
Hughes Field, Howard (Houston, Texas), 62–63

Irimeseu, Radu, 35
Itasco (ship), 46

Jacqueline Cochran Cosmetic
    Company. See Cochran
    Cosmetic Company, Jacqueline
Joe (foster brother), 3
Johnson, Lyndon B., 80

Kennedy, John F., 96

Lerton, Mrs., 22–23
Liberty magazine, 70–74
Life magazine, 94
Lindbergh, Charles, 30
Little, Brown and Company, 82
Lockheed, 98–99
    F-104 Starfighter, 99
    Hudson bombers, 51, 52
    Lodestar airplane, 97, 100
Love, Nancy Harkness, 61–62, 66
Lovelace, Randy, 97

Mach 1 (speed of sound), 92–96
Mach 2, 99
MacRobertson Race (1934) from
    London, England, to Mel-
    bourne, Australia, 32–36
Mamie (foster sister), 3, 5, 16
Manhattan, Jackie and Floyd's
    apartment in, 43, 54, 56, 78,
    84
Mao Tse-tung, 72
Marshall, Ted, 31
Miami Beach, Florida, Jackie's life
    in, 26, 28–29
Mildenhall Field (London), 34
Monroe, Marilyn, 76
Montgomery, Alabama, Jackie's life
    in, 22–23

Mother, Jackie's foster, 1, 5–7, 9,
    15–17, 19–20, 26
Myrtle (foster sister), 3, 5

NASA (National Aeronautics and
    Space Administration), 97–98
NATO (North Atlantic Treaty
    Organization), 83
New York City, Jackie's life in, 25–
    26, 29
    Antoine's Salon at Saks Fifth
        Avenue, 26, 29, 43–44
    apartment in Manhattan, 43, 54,
        56, 78, 84
    cosmetic business moves to
        Rockefeller Center, 43–44
New York Journal-American, 82
Ninety-Niners, 44
Noonan, Fred, 44, 46
Northrop
    Gamma airplane, 37, 38, 40–41
    T-38 airplane, 96
Nuremberg trials, 73

Odlum, Floyd B., 8, 46, 51, 70,
    72, 87, 88, 102, 104
    Canadair and, 90–91
    death of, 103
    Eisenhower's 1952 presidential
        campaign and, 84–85
    health of, 75, 78, 100, 101
    Jackie's autobiography supported
        and encouraged by, 82
    Jackie's congressional candidacy
        privately opposed by, 86
    Jackie's cosmetic business sup-
        ported and encouraged by, 37

Odlum, Floyd B. (*cont'd*)
  Jackie's flying career supported
    and encouraged by, 29–
    32, 39, 44, 75–76, 92, 97
  meets Jackie, 28–29
  Office of Production Manage-
    ment and, 56
  space medical research, support
    for, 97
  weds Jackie, 42–43
  World War II and, 55–56
Odlum, Jacqueline Cochran. *See*
  Cochran, Jacqueline
Odlum, Victor, 72
Office of Production Management,
  56

P-35 pursuit plane, 46
P-51 airplane, 75, 76
Paramount Pictures, 94
Pensacola, Florida, Jackie's life in,
  24
"Perk Up," 78
Pittman, Bessie Lee, 7
Pius XII, Pope, 72–73
Pratt and Whitney engine, 37
Putnam, George, 44

Quod Erat Demonstradum
  (Q.E.D.) airplane, 33

Reza Shah Pahlavi (Shah of Iran),
  72
Richler, Mrs., 19, 21–23
Ringling Brothers Circus, 8
Rockefeller Center, 43–44
Romanian Air Ministry, 35

Roosevelt, Eleanor, 57, 61
Roosevelt, Franklin D., 54–57, 68,
  69
Roosevelt Field (Long Island,
  N.Y.), 30
Rosen, Mickey, 30

Saks Fifth Avenue, Antoine's Salon
  at, 26, 29, 43–44
San Diego Union, 81–82
Savoy Hotel (London), 59
Seversky, Alexander P. de, 46, 48
Seversky airplane, 46, 48
Shah of Iran (Reza Shah Pahlavi),
  72
Sharp, Evelyn, 67
Smith, Wesley, 33–35
Sound, speed of (Mach 1), 92–96
Stars at Noon, The (Jackie's autobi-
  ography), 82
Stevenson, Adlai, 84–85

T-33 jet trainer, 91
T-38 airplane, 96
Tarter, Aldine, 101–2
Travelair airplane, 31

U.S. Air Force, 62, 91, 96
  Academy, 103, 104
  Distinguished Flying Cross, 100
  Reserve, 89
U.S. Army
  Air Corps, 46
  Air Force, 51
  training methods, 63–64
U.S. Congress
  bill to militarize WASPs, 67, 68

U.S. Congress (*cont'd*)
Jackie's unsuccessful candidacy,
85–86
U.S. Department of State, 53
U.S. Ferry Command, 61
U.S. Navy, 31, 97–98
University of Colorado Law School,
28

Webb, James, 97
Willebrandt, Mabel, 33, 36
Willie Mae (Mamie's daughter), 16
Women's Airforce Service Pilots
(WASP), 66–68, 70
Women's Auxiliary Flying Service
(WAFS), 61–62, 66
Women's Flying Training Detach-
ment, 62–64, 66

Women's National Aeronautical
Association, 46
World War II, 83
Floyd and, 55–56
Jackie and, 50–64, 66–74
Wright, Orville, 89
Wright, Wilbur, 89

X-1 research rocket, 89

Yeager, Charles (Chuck)
Congressional Medal of Honor
awarded to, 90
Jackie's friendship with, 89–97,
100
Yeager, Glennis, 90